The Next Generation of STEM Teachers

The Next Generation of STEM Teachers

An Interdisciplinary Approach to Meet the Needs of the Future

Edited by
Patrick M. Jenlink and Karen Embry Jenlink

ROWMAN & LITTLEFIELD
Lanham • Boulder • New York • London

Published by Rowman & Littlefield
An imprint of The Rowman & Littlefield Publishing Group, Inc.
4501 Forbes Boulevard, Suite 200, Lanham, Maryland 20706
www.rowman.com

6 Tinworth Street, London SE11 5AL, United Kingdom

Copyright © 2019 by Patrick M. Jenlink and Karen Embry Jenlink

All rights reserved. No part of this book may be reproduced in any form or by any electronic or mechanical means, including information storage and retrieval systems, without written permission from the publisher, except by a reviewer who may quote passages in a review.

British Library Cataloguing in Publication Information Available

Library of Congress Cataloging-in-Publication Data

Names: Jenlink, Patrick M., editor. | Embry Jenlink, Karen, 1959- editor.
Title: The next generation of STEM teachers : an interdisciplinary approach to meet the needs of the future / edited by Patrick M. Jenlink and Karen Embry Jenlink.
Description: Lanham, Maryland : Roman & Littlefield, 2019. | Includes bibliographical references.
Identifiers: LCCN 2018057346 (print) | LCCN 2019005542 (ebook) | ISBN 9781475822762 | ISBN 9781475822748 (cloth : alk. paper) | ISBN 9781475822755 (pbk. : alk. paper)
Subjects: LCSH: Science teachers—Training of. | Mathematics teachers—Training of. | Science—Study and teaching. | Mathematics—Study and teaching.
Classification: LCC Q181 (ebook) | LCC Q181 .N397 2019 (print) | DDC 507.1/2—dc23
LC record available at https://lccn.loc.gov/2018057346

∞™ The paper used in this publication meets the minimum requirements of American National Standard for Information Sciences—Permanence of Paper for Printed Library Materials, ANSI/NISO Z39.48-1992.

Printed in the United States of America

To the future generations of STEM educators and students.

Contents

Preface ix

Acknowledgments xiii

1 STEM Teacher Preparation and Practice: An Interdisciplinary Perspective 1
Patrick M. Jenlink and Karen Embry Jenlink

PART I: INTERDISCIPLINARY THINKING AND PLACE-BASED PRACTICES IN STEM 15

2 Toward an Eccentric Educational Ideal: The Demands for Interdisciplinary Thinking and Collaboration 19
Shawn Vecellio

3 Looking Deeper through the STEM Lens: Exploring the Intersection between Content and Context to Optimize STEM Learning 35
Louis S. Nadelson and Anne L. Seifert

4 "I Don't Know Anything about DNA. Well I Do, but Not from You Guys": A Vision for Interdisciplinary STEM Teaching 51
Vanessa Svihla, Kersti Tyson, Justin Boyle, Jamie Collins, Ara Winter, Ayesha Livingston, Abigail Stiles, and Julie Bryant

5 Mathematics, Science, and Technology Reform in Teacher Education: Implications for Teaching Practice 69
Deborah Moore-Russo and Noemi Waight

PART II: COMPLEXITIES AND CHALLENGES IN STEM EDUCATION — 87

6 Developing a STEM Education Teacher Preparation Program to Help Increase STEM Literacy among Preservice Teachers — 93
Margaret Mohr-Schroeder, Christa Jackson, D. Craig Schroeder, and Jennifer Wilhelm

7 Troubling STEM: Making a Case for an Ethics and STEM Partnership — 113
Astrid Steele

8 Preparing Science Teaching Candidates to Deliver Language-Rich STEM Instruction — 131
Kevin Carr and Jonathan Pope

9 Promoting an Interdisciplinary Approach to STEM Education: Matching STEM Pedagogy to Trends on the Demand Side — 147
Joseph Mukuni

10 Epilogue: The Future of STEM Teaching — 157
Patrick M. Jenlink and Karen Embry Jenlink

About the Editors — 163

About the Contributors — 165

Preface

Increasingly, attention is focused on improving science, technology, engineering, and math (STEM) education in the United States as well as on the global stage; this attention is concerned with meeting the needs of rapidly changing domestic and global societies. Simultaneously, there is a growing discourse focused on an interdisciplinary approach to STEM education within public schools and teacher-preparation programs in colleges and universities. The emphasis on interdisciplinary STEM includes integration within STEM disciplines or across and between STEM and non-STEM disciplines.

Historically, academic disciplines have often been isolated, working within metaphorical silos. An academic discipline is often understood to imply a distinctive way of making knowledge; making knowledge, in the case of STEM, refers to making knowledge in the different sciences (e.g., biology, physics, chemistry, astronomy, etc.) as well as in mathematics, engineering, and technology. In this sense, making knowledge is all too often viewed as taking place within silos. But making knowledge can mean much more than this, such as making knowledge within STEM education that works to make disciplinary boundaries more permeable and enables individuals to work in an interdisciplinary fashion to solve complex problems that a singular discipline is unable to solve extant from other bodies of knowledge.

Disciplinarity can imply a field of deep and detailed content knowledge within complex and ever-changing social and cultural as well as multidimensional contexts, a community of professional practice that gains advantage by brokering knowledge creation and use across what has historically been disciplinary knowledge within silos, a form of creative and innovative discourse, an area of work (such as an academic department or a research area), a domain of public access to new knowledge and public communication emphasizing the importance of interdisciplinary knowledge, a site of learning where individuals are inducted into a cross-disciplinary modalities of learning and knowledge creation, a method of reading and analyzing the complexities of the world, a systemic frame or way of thinking—even a way of acting and a type of person.

The interdisciplinary nature of the world in which we live and work demands a broadening of STEM education and literacy. The more traditional meaning of *literacy* in the modern society conveys "basic" levels of competency in reading and writing. *Literacy* in the sense of STEM literacy reflects multimodal literacies aligned with the disciplinarity of science, technology, engineering, and mathematics. Interdisciplinary STEM gives a new meaning to STEM literacy. STEM literacy is an interdisciplinary area of study that interweaves the four areas of science, technology, engineering, and mathematics. STEM literacy does not simply mean achieving literacy in these four strands or silos; rather it means transcending existing boundaries and creating paths of communication and knowledge that heretofore have not existed.

Preparing STEM-literate teachers in the interdisciplinary sense reflects a level of multimodal literacy, meaning that it is no longer enough for literacy to focus solely on the rules of standard forms of knowledge and disciplinary language. Rather, an interdisciplinary communication and representation of STEM learning and teaching today increasingly requires that teachers become able to negotiate differences in patterns of meaning from one disciplinary knowledge to another and from one context to another. In this sense, STEM literacy as directly related to creating and communicating knowledge across disciplinary boundaries reflects a form of interdisciplinary pedagogy.

The importance and relevance of this interdisciplinary perspective to teacher preparation lies in the realization that STEM literacy moves into everyday lives and thinking and not just in STEM-related disciplines. Integrating STEM literacy in teacher preparation is the notion that preparation includes approaches that explore teaching and learning between and among two or more STEM subject areas. This means that faculty in teacher preparation need to extend the range of STEM literacy in pedagogical strategies so that STEM teaching is enriched with multimodal literacies into teaching and learning, which in turn makes STEM knowledge more relevant and engaging for its manifest connections to solving the problems that challenge society.

The purpose of *The Next Generation of STEM Teachers: An Interdisciplinary Approach to Meet the Needs of the Future* is to break from the more historical idea of making knowledge within disciplines and to engage the reader in a growing conversation that is gaining momentum and is focused on an "interdisciplinarity of STEM education," which seeks to embrace or present emerging perspectives on the standards. Importantly, the conversation on STEM education and interdisciplinary approaches to teacher preparation may draw into specific relief the respective professional or disciplinary standards for each of the four STEM disciplines as each relates to fostering an interdisciplinary approach.

As a point of clarification related to an at-times overused and ill-defined concept, interdisciplinary work is grounded in the historical practices of more than one discipline and consciously crosses disciplinary contexts and boundaries; interdisciplinarity makes the disciplinary silos of knowledge permeable and enables boundary crossing that works to solve complex problems, while at the same time working to create an environment for creativity and innovation needed to meet the challenges of an ever-changing world and advance new and much-needed problem-based ways of addressing the challenges both present and yet to be experienced.

Legacy notions of "teaching" that have defined teacher practice and preparation, which often pass from teacher educators to the next generation of STEM teachers, need to be replaced by new notions of "interdisciplinary learning." This interdisciplinarity is necessary to advance the idea of crossing disciplinary boundaries through interdisciplinary communities of practice defined by intellectual discourse and place- and project-based learning rather than the traditional, instrumental role of teachers of the recent past, defined by narrowly delimited standards and testable outcomes. Interdisciplinary learning is a vital pedagogical strategy for engaging the increasingly complex challenges teachers face today and the equally complex and dynamic solutions needed to address these challenges. Such interdisciplinary learning coalesces around STEM and the realization that the challenges confronting education and society today require a radically different, re-envisioned science, technology, engineering, and mathematics education, which are needed to provide a foundational STEM education for the immediate problems facing society and the problems yet to be born as society continually evolves.

STEM education benefits from both the deeper perspectives of disciplinary work, with work that has historically taken place within silos, as well as the need for STEM education to be balanced with and measured against the broader perspectives of science, technology, engineering, and mathematics that can only be accomplished through interdisciplinarity. Preparing STEM teachers for STEM classrooms in schools requires interdisciplinary approaches that are applied, for reasons of principle, to disrupt the habitual narrowness of outlook of within-discipline knowledge work and to challenge the ingrained, discipline-bound ways of thinking that produce occlusion as well as insight. Preparing a next-generation STEM teacher can no longer rest on past efforts or be limited by a standards-based perspective that is in and of itself bound in silos. Interdisciplinary approaches to STEM will thrive within the interface of disciplinary and lay understandings, bringing the worlds of knowledge making and of the public closer together. There is agreement that the practical application of disciplined understandings is necessary, and there is emerging understanding of the practical application of interdisciplinary understandings as necessary to address the problems existing in the world. Much intellectual and practical work at some point requires disciplinarians—mathematicians, engineers, scientists, and technology specialists—to become interdisciplinarians. Education in general and teacher education, in particular, are cases in point.

The Next Generation of STEM Teachers offers a primary focus on STEM teaching, interdisciplinary STEM, and integrating the disciplinary discourse to create a new vista of STEM education. Following an introductory chapter, Part I presents the first four chapters (2–5), which reflect discourses on the eccentric educational ideal of STEM interdisciplinarity, the intersection between STEM content knowledge and context, a vision of interdisciplinary STEM teaching, and implications of interdisciplinary STEM for teaching practice. In Part II, the next set of chapters (6–9) focus on the complexities and challenges in STEM education, STEM literacy, ethics in STEM partnerships, integration and teaching though an interdisciplinary lens/perspective, STEM pedagogy, advancing ideas for creating STEAM from STEM, and the nuances of STEM education in teacher preparation. The epilogue provides a summary of the preceding chapters and gives a sense of future direction.

Acknowledgments

This volume has been three years in coming to fruition. The initial idea for this project began as a conversation focused on the nature of STEM education and what worked and did not and why. We recognized that STEM disciplines remained in silos and that teachers who were prepared in these disciplinary silos had a distinct disadvantage to understanding the complexity of STEM education and that we needed to advance new perspectives of STEM education that were interdisciplinary in nature. Perhaps one of the telling points in the conversations was the realization that in the STEM workforce, new, advanced interdisciplinary perspectives were shaping how the workforce approached problems and challenges in innovations and advancements across a broad spectrum of applications in all aspects of society.

Over time, and through the course of a series of conversations with colleagues on issues of STEM education, teaching, and teacher preparation, always focusing inward on how STEM education and the role of STEM teachers and current research in STEM education informed current perspectives, the realization that new, fresh perspectives that transcended disciplinary silos in teacher preparation were needed. As well, these conversations offered possibilities for new perspectives in preparing a reimagined and decidedly advanced teacher preparation programs that would, in turn, prepare a new generation of STEM teachers needed in shaping education for the future.

Like others who have written on STEM teacher preparation, we believe that STEM teacher preparation is quintessential to advancing K–12 teaching and learning for our public schools, colleges, and universities. We believe that interwoven with an interdisciplinary perspective of STEM teacher preparation is a need for creative and collaborative ways of advancing place-based and integrative approaches to STEM education in concert with the STEM workforce.

Equally important, based on our conversations, we believe that the structured disciplinary silos are a tradition of the past that must now be set aside, and new, interdisciplinary ways of approaching STEM education must be embraced. Academic disciplines and what takes place within the public space of schools today, as well as the structure of the university, largely influences the shaping of STEM education. Therein lies the realization that past traditions of teaching and teacher preparation must now be replaced with new visions of STEM of interdisciplinary teaching and learning that will lead to STEM education becoming a meta-discipline.

First, we wish to thank the contributing authors whose experience in the day-to-day work of preparing teachers offered insight and thoughtful considerations for understanding interdisciplinary STEM teacher preparation juxtaposed with the difficult struggles for advancing a concentrated focus on the invaluable role that STEM education plays in society today. Although theorists and researchers have written extensively on STEM education across the years, it is often the voices of the teacher educators in the university classrooms and colleges, working with the preservice preparation students of teaching, that bring clarity to understanding the complexity of interdisciplinarity in relation to STEM knowledge, pedagogy, integration, and the need to move away from the traditional models of teacher preparation and toward an interdisciplinary, place-based model that enables each new generation of STEM teachers to enter K–12 classrooms equipped to teach STEM education to our next generation of STEM professionals, innovators, and educators.

The authors of the chapters examining STEM teacher preparation in Part II of the book brought their considerable experience to bear on interpreting the complexity, challenges, and problems associated with reimagining STEM teacher preparation through an interdisciplinary lens. It is also important to note that the authors represent the voices of STEM teacher preparation faculty and researchers that give presence of mind to the importance of understanding STEM education and STEM teacher preparation as a critical factor in meeting the needs of a STEM-rich society and its educational system.

Second, we would like to express our gratitude to the external reviewers who took time out of their busy schedules to review and provide comments and suggestions. Acknowledging the value of the chapters and offering constructive feedback were invaluable, as was the affirmation by reviewers for both the need and importance of a book committed to STEM teacher preparation.

Third, we would like to thank Tom Koerner, Carlie Wall, and the editorial staff at Rowman & Littlefield for their vision in seeing the value of a book on interdisciplinary STEM teacher preparation that draws into specific relief the need to advance interdisciplinary perspectives of STEM education and the need to prepare a new generation of teachers that embrace interdisciplinarity. As well, we would like to thank the production staff at Rowman & Littlefield for their ever-vigilant efforts to move the book through to completion. Working with a quality publisher and the folks that do the work to translate a manuscript into a completed book is a rewarding experience.

Fourth, we would like to extend appreciation to Son Pham, our doctoral research assistant, who worked diligently with us to proofread and ensure a high-quality manuscript. His dedication to the quality of the book manuscript is beyond compare.

Finally, we would like to recognize our institution, Stephen F. Austin State University, for supporting this project and enabling the realization of a work that we believe will further an important and much-needed discourse concerned with STEM teacher preparation—meeting the challenges and problems associated with interdisciplinary perspectives of teaching and learning STEM education in schools across the United States.

Chapter 1

STEM Teacher Preparation and Practice

An Interdisciplinary Perspective

Patrick M. Jenlink and Karen Embry Jenlink

Substantial attention is now focused on improving science, technology, engineering, and math (STEM) education in the United States and internationally.[1] If we are to advance STEM integration in teacher preparation and in the teaching of STEM curriculum in K–12 classrooms in ways that reflect nuanced epistemological and pedagogical perspectives, STEM teacher educators need to focus on both core content knowledge and interdisciplinary processes as a foundation for preparing STEM educators.

As evidenced in numerous articles, interdisciplinary approaches to STEM education are emblematic of a rapidly emerging perspective that has direct bearing on reimagining STEM teacher preparation programs (e.g., Burke, Francis, & Shanahan, 2014; Fioriello, 2010; Honey, Pearson, & Schweingruber, 2014; Moore & Smith, 2014; Rennie, Wallace, & Venville, 2012; Traphagen & Traill, 2014; Vasquez, Sneider, & Comer, 2013).

A well-grounded argument has been made that for STEM education, at both PK–12 and higher-education levels, to be successful in meeting the needs of a rapidly changing society, both domestically and globally,[2] for the present and the future, will require a new integrative and interdisciplinary perspective that provides a clear articulation between PK–12 and higher education (Kalantzis & Cope, 2014), and in particular. between teacher preparation and the day-to-day work of STEM teaching in classrooms.[3]

What we know is that teachers are one of the most critical elements in the STEM learning ecosystem.[4] What we also know is that STEM teacher educators will need to shift from a more traditional perspective of teacher preparation to an interdisciplinary perspective that views STEM teaching as boundary-crossing and integrative in nature (Stillman & Anderson, 2014).

This chapter examines the current status of STEM education in relation to teacher preparation and practice. As an introduction to the book, emphasis will be placed on the importance of STEM integration, which may include integration within STEM disciplines or across and between STEM and non-STEM disciplines. The authors advance an interdisciplinary perspective and acknowledge the importance of preparing STEM-literate teachers for schools and classrooms, as well as the need for STEM literacy in advancing a preK–16 bridge to the future of US education and innovation.

INTERDISCIPLINARITY IN TEACHER PREPARATION

The interdisciplinary nature of the world in which we live and work demands a broadening of STEM education and research (Fioriello, 2010; Hoachlander, 2014/2015). Interdisciplinary approaches to STEM research are emerging in the literature; however, the presence of STEM integration as a distinct field of study is in its infant stages (Honey et al., 2014).

Interdisciplinary STEM teacher preparation can change the paradigm of what teaching is, and in turn, interdisciplinary STEM teaching can change the conventional paradigm of the classroom as a learning environment for students. Teachers become the facilitators of interdisciplinary learning, while students discover, explore, design, and question. The nature of complex problems and place-based learning become the context for experiential learning that is guided by integrated knowledge and pedagogically enriched activities. STEM teachers create multidimensional learning scenarios, supportive of critical thinking and designing solutions that are relevant to the real world.

STEM Teacher Educators

Changing the paradigm from one of disciplinary perspective to interdisciplinary perspectives of teacher preparation presents challenges (Ledbetter, 2012; Read, 2013). STEM teacher educators must understand and embrace that there are various important but complex problems, phenomena, and concepts that resist understanding or resolution when approached from single disciplines. This understanding of the complexity of problems is a critical part of how to translate interdisciplinary teaching in learning experiences, wherein preservice teacher candidates are situated to interrogate, understand, and explore solutions they design based on their integration and application of various disciplinary knowledges.

Given the complexity of working across multiple ways of knowing and different disciplinary perspectives, the STEM teacher educator will find interdisciplinary subjects challenging to teach (Stillman & Anderson, 2014).

Equally challenging is the articulation of interdisciplinarity into epistemological and pedagogical approaches to preparing the preservice teacher–candidate. And STEM preservice teacher–candidates will find interdisciplinary knowledge a challenge to learn.

Therefore, STEM teacher preparation faculty will need to understand interdisciplinarity in its complexity to engage preservice teacher–candidates epistemologically and pedagogically in ways of learning that engage the candidates in learning interdisciplinarity. Candidates will need interdisciplinary perspectives, knowledges, skills, attitudes, and understandings, and they will need to learn interdisciplinary ways of teaching, learning the integrative structures that enable interdisciplinary teaching and learning (Golding, 2009). Teaching the preservice candidates in STEM preparation programs, these integrative structures are essential as they are unlikely to have learned the structures previously, given the concentration on disciplinary teaching in much of the educational system.

STEM Preservice Teacher–Candidates

Interdisciplinary STEM preservice teacher–candidates must learn to interrogate multiple ways of knowing and the structure of knowledge itself, not only knowledge within a single discipline but knowledge that is integrated from multiple disciplines. The preservice teacher–candidate must develop a reflective and explicit knowledge of how disciplines work, the issues and problems they can address, and "the strengths and limitations of each discipline as well as the possibilities of interaction between them" (Boix Mansilla, Miller, & Gardner, 2000, p. 36).

Equally important, preservice teacher–candidates must have and understand explicit knowledge of how interdisciplinary perspectives of various knowledges and the application of these knowledges enable them to approach a complex problem in a place-based context with new levels of thinking and understanding.

STEM Teaching and Learning

For successful interdisciplinary teaching and learning, STEM teacher preparation faculty must have conceptions about the nature of interdisciplinarity and its application to epistemology and pedagogy. Teacher educators will need sophisticated conceptions of multiple knowledges, within and across disciplinary boundaries, to make sense of the multiple and often-contrary disciplinary perspectives that they will be engaging the preservice teacher–candidate within an interdisciplinary STEM curriculum (Golding, 2009; Rennie et al., 2012). Without these conceptions, preservice teacher–candidates will misunderstand the whole endeavor of interdisciplinary teaching and learning, and they will end up frustrated and distracted from their responsibility of teaching students (Golding, 2009).

REIMAGINING STEM EDUCATION

Preparing STEM teachers for STEM classrooms in schools requires interdisciplinary approaches that are applied, for reasons of principle, to disrupt the habitual narrowness of outlook of within-discipline knowledge work and to challenge the ingrained, discipline-bound ways of thinking that produce occlusion as well as insight (Golding, 2009; Werth, 2003). Preparing a next-generation STEM teacher can no longer rest on past efforts or be limited by a standards-based perspective that is in and of itself bound in silos.

Reimagining STEM education begins, in part, with reimagining STEM teacher preparation. Reimagining traditional teacher preparation as interdisciplinary STEM teacher preparation will require addressing new perspectives of STEM literacy, integration, curricula, and pedagogy, which are guided by interdisciplinary perspectives that give rise to a STEM architecture.[5]

STEM Literacy

Nobel laureate physicist and founder of the Illinois Mathematics and Science Academy, Leon Lederman (1998) defined "STEM literacy" as the ability to adapt to and accept changes driven by new technologies and innovations within and across other disciplines, to anticipate the multilevel impacts of their actions, communicate complex ideas effectively to a variety of audiences, and perhaps most importantly, find "measured yet creative solutions to problems which are today unimaginable" (p. 4).

STEM literacy is an interdisciplinary area of study that bridges the four areas of science, technology, engineering, and mathematics into a comprehensive and coherent curricula across content areas. STEM literacy includes, but does not simply mean, achieving independent literacy in these four strands or silos; rather, STEM literacy focuses on relevant integration alongside independent literacy. Consequently, a STEM classroom shifts students away from learning discrete bits and pieces of phenomenon and rote procedures toward investigating and questioning the interrelated facets of the world (Kalantzis & Cope, 2014; Morrison, 2006).

Other authors have defined:

> STEM literacy is central to fostering engaged citizenship, rewarding employment, and ultimately to improve social, environmental and economic

conditions in local and global communities. Moreover, ensuring that individuals and communities that have historically been underserved and overlooked are STEM-capable can put an end to cycles of poverty and provides access to a brighter future. This means that now, more than ever, being well prepared in STEM is essential for all our nation's students—those seeking employment immediately following high school completion, those bound for community colleges or universities, as well as those pursing STEM professions. (Milliken & Adams, 2010, p. 14)

STEM literacy requires intentionally making the connections across subjects where appropriate. It requires a pedagogical shift in instruction that connects learning to students' own interests and experiences and connects students to real-world problems and learning opportunities. STEM teaching wherein STEM literacy is key is concerned with learning that is equitable, providing all students the opportunities to learn, develop, and acquire skills that will provide success in life.

Importantly, interdisciplinarity in preservice teacher-preparation programs advances the need, on the part of the STEM preservice teacher–candidates, to learn how to occupy different disciplinary perspectives and to talk critically but reasonably across these perspectives. They need to be able to comprehend and translate disciplinary languages, ways of knowing and methods, and then balance, synthesize, and integrate them (Felix & Harris, 2010).

STEM Integration

STEM teaching and learning requires cross-disciplinary collaboration. Carroll and Foster (2010) argued that to meet the needs of today's STEM learners, the tradition of artisan teaching in solo-practice classrooms will give way to a school culture in which teachers continuously develop their content knowledge and pedagogical skills in collaborative practice that is embedded in the daily fabric of their work. Teacher collaboration supports student learning, and the good news is that teachers who work in strong learning communities are more satisfied with their careers and are more likely to remain in teaching long enough to become accomplished teachers (Huber & Hutchings, 2005).

Based on Virginia Tech's Integrative Science, Technology, Engineering, and Mathematics (STEM) Education degree program launched in 2006, Wells and Ernst (2012 as cited in Wells, 2013, p. 29) defined integrative STEM education as

> the application of technological/engineering design-based pedagogical approaches to *intentionally* teach content and practices of science and mathematics education concurrently with content and practices of technology/engineering education. Integrative STEM education is equally applicable at the

natural intersections of learning within the continuum of content areas, educational environments, and academic levels. (sec. 1)

Virginia Tech's program, the first of its kind in the United States, serves as an exemplar of a STEM-integration paradigm for preparing twenty-first–century educators, leaders, scholars, and researchers prepared to investigate, teach, and disseminate new integrative approaches to STEM education. The integrative STEM education program serves as the theoretical and pedagogical premise for technological/engineering (T/E) design-based teaching and learning practices.

The goal of T/E design-based learning is distinct in that it seeks to promote integrative STEM thinking. T/E design embodies habits of both hand and mind that together afford the learner the knowledge and understanding necessary for developing appropriate solutions to human wants and needs (Virginia Tech, n.d.).

Crossing disciplinary boundaries is a primary feature of integrated STEM perspectives. Honey et al. (2014), in their National Academies Press report, *STEM Integration in K–12 Education: Status, Prospects, and an Agenda for Research*, provided a basic definition of integration as "working in the context of complex phenomena or situations on tasks that require students to use knowledge and skills from multiple disciplines" (p. 52).

Different forms of boundary crossing are displayed along a continuum of increasing levels of integration, with progression along the continuum involving greater interconnection and interdependence among the disciplines; disciplinary boundary crossing is an interdisciplinary process that enables the STEM teacher to create place-based, experiential learning for students (English, 2016; English & Gainsburg, 2016; Moore & Smith, 2014; Vasquez et al., 2013). The *STEM Task Force Report* (2014) adopts the view that STEM education is far more than a "convenient integration" of its four disciplines, rather it encompasses "real-world, problem-based learning" that links the disciplines "through cohesive and active teaching and learning approaches" (p. 9).

STEM Curricula

Preservice teacher–candidates who engage in a STEM curriculum focused on place-based learning and solving complex problems in a real-world scenario will need interdisciplinary collaboration skills if they are to work in cross-disciplinary teams, disciplinary interpretation, and synthesis skills if they are personally integrating information from multiple disciplines (Morrison, 2006).

Whereas higher education plays an important role in preparing students within different academic disciplines for careers in STEM, equally important is the role that STEM teacher preparation plays in preparing teachers to enter the K–12 classroom. For this reason, K–12 education and higher education must work jointly in designing integrative and collaborative relationships guided by interdisciplinary perspectives that work to eliminate disciplinary silos (Duschl & Bismack, 2016; Duschl, Bismack, Greeno, & Gitomer, 2016; Kalantzis & Cope, 2014; Rennie et al., 2012).

Learning in the STEM disciplines is experiential, placed-based, and focused on interdisciplinary perspectives. An authentic STEM curriculum provides points of integration among multiple STEM disciplines and fosters innovation. STEM courses should provide students with opportunities to innovate and produce, both individually and collaboratively, through real-world applications and projects. These courses should also provide students with engaging, hands-on, and relevant experiences that build logical and quantitative reasoning. Currently, this is not uniformly expected in science, technology, engineering, and mathematics classrooms.

Building STEM courses requires more attention to the "instructional" elements of the classroom than it does the "curricular." Teachers should encourage students to question and investigate, cultivating a critical questioning, instead of allowing them to rely on rote procedures. They should require students to complete projects that require problem solving in placed-based settings, instead of relying on worksheets. They should encourage students to be creative, instead of emphasizing a simple application of procedures. Finally, they should teach students to work collaboratively in teams, instead of assuming this automatically happens when students work in groups.

STEM Pedagogy

As the President's Council of Advisors on Science and Technology (PCAST) Report (2010), *Prepare and Inspire: K–12 Education in Science, Technology, Engineering, and Math (STEM) for America's Future*, stated, "Teachers are the single most important factor in the K–12 education system" (p. 57). The report further stated, "Great STEM teachers have at least two attributes: deep content knowledge in STEM, and strong pedagogical skills for teaching their students STEM" (p. 57).

STEM pedagogies in teacher preparation that are reflective of the qualities derived from STEM disciplines, including cognitive skills, critical questioning, aesthetic appreciation, innovative and creative design, and social interaction, are necessary to advancing a new paradigm of STEM teaching.

Interdisciplinary curricula and pedagogies that integrate disciplinary subjects are pivotal for preparing the interdisciplinary STEM preservice teacher–candidates, teaching them how to understand, navigate, and employ multiple, and often contrary, ways of knowing. Situating preservice teacher–candidates in these interdisciplinary curricula enables them to develop a meta-knowledge about different disciplines, methods, and epistemologies and learn how to purposefully and reflectively integrate and synthesize different perspectives to advance understanding and solve problems.

For successful interdisciplinary teaching and learning, STEM teacher preparation faculty must have conceptions about the nature of interdisciplinarity and its application to epistemology and pedagogy. Teacher educators will need sophisticated conceptions of multiple knowledges, within and across disciplinary boundaries, to make sense of the multiple and often contrary disciplinary perspectives that they will be engaging the preservice teacher–candidate within an interdisciplinary STEM curriculum. The need for sophisticated conceptions of multiple knowledges requires equally sophisticated conceptions of STEM pedagogies derived from the STEM disciplines and imagined[6] through the lens of interdisciplinarity.

CONCLUSIONS

Teacher-preparation programs must also be reimagined to develop a new generation of STEM educators. To aid STEM teachers as they meet the challenge of teaching in the field of STEM, the STEM teacher educators must begin to rework their teacher-preparation programs and how they address professional development.

Preparing STEM teachers to enter classrooms to teach STEM disciplines guided by interdisciplinary perspectives will require much work in rearticulating teacher preparation to align with the needs of a changing global society. The increasing reality of a STEM-based workforce and knowledge economy offers great challenges, ever-present tensions, and transformative possibilities for teacher preparation and the teaching profession. Preparing STEM-literate teachers is directly linked to the success of preparing STEM-literate students.

Larson (2013) argued what is perhaps the most important point concerning STEM education and importance of preparing STEM teachers:

> Becoming knowledgeable about STEM is not about the 0.01% who might become PhD researchers or the 1% who might become engineers. In this data-informed, technology intensive [twenty-first century] the entire populace needs to become STEM literate. We all need STEM thinking skills . . . the most

important reason for everyone to become STEM literate is to build a more informed citizenry. In that way we individually and collectively become better decision makers about all the options that our world and we face. STEM is not only for PhD researchers. It's for all of us! (para. 12)

NOTES

1. Nations that enjoy high international testing outcomes as well as strong STEM agendas have well-developed curricula that concentrate on twenty-first–century skills, including inquiry processes, problem solving, critical thinking, creativity, and innovation as well as a strong focus on disciplinary knowledge (English & Gainsburg, 2016; Marginson et al., 2013; Partnership for 21st Century Skills, 2011). The need to nurture generic skills, in-depth conceptual understandings, and their interdisciplinary connections is paramount.

2. Although domestic and international interest in STEM from educational and workforce perspectives has proliferated in recent years, the acronym was coined in the United States during the 1990s by the National Science Foundation. The combining of the disciplines was seen as "a strategic decision made by scientists, technologists, engineers, and mathematicians to combine forces and create a stronger political voice" (STEM Task Force Report, 2014, p. 9).

3. See Bybee (2010); Davies and Devlin (2007); Felix and Harris (2010); Golding (2009); Kaufman et al. (2003); King (2011); Larson (2013); Ledbetter 2012; Morrison (2006); National Academy of Education (2009); National Research Council (NRC; 2011); The NEA Foundation (2012); President's Council of Advisors on Science and Technology (PCAST, 2010); Read (2013); Sanders (2008, 2012, 2013); Traphagen and Traill (2014); Tsupros et al. (2009); and Wilson (2011, 2013).

4. Traphagen and Traill (2014) defined a STEM learning ecosystem as one that "encompasses schools, community settings such as after-school and summer programs, science centers and museums, and informal experiences at home and in a variety of environments that together constitute a rich array of learning opportunities for young people. A learning ecosystem harnesses the unique contributions of all these different settings in symbiosis to deliver STEM learning for all children. Designed pathways enable young people to become engaged, knowledgeable and skilled in the STEM disciplines as they progress through childhood into adolescence and early adulthood" (p. 4).

5. Architecture, as used in relation to STEM, conveys a set of meta-patterns, broad in nature, a set of "overarching patterns that span multiple contexts (e.g., academic disciplines, cultures, personal experiences, etc.), and are transphenomenal and transdisciplinary. . . . Although context-specific meanings of each metapattern may differ, the essential core meanings or functions are shared across such contexts" (Volk & Bloom, 2007, p. 46).

6. Albert Einstein's (1931) belief in imagination extends into reimagining teacher preparation that embraces in interdisciplinary perspective, which enables us to step

beyond the traditional boundaries of knowledge: "Imagination is more important than knowledge. For knowledge is limited to all we now know and understand, while imagination embraces the entire world, and all there ever will be to know and understand" (p. 97).

REFERENCES

Boix Mansilla, V., Gardner, H., & Miller, W. (2000). On disciplinary lenses and interdisciplinary work. In S. Wineburg & P. Grossman (Eds.), *Interdisciplinary curriculum: Challenges to implementation* (pp. 17–38). New York: Teacher College Press.

Burke, L., Francis, K., & Shanahan, M. (2014). A horizon of possibilities: A definition of stem education. Paper presented at the STEM 2014 Conference, Vancouver, British Columbia, Canada, July 12–15.

Bybee, R. W. (2010). Advancing STEM education: A 2020 vision. *Technology and Engineering Teacher, 70*(1), 30–35.

Carroll, T., & Foster, E. (2010). *Who will teach? Experience matters.* Washington, DC: NCTAF. Retrieved November 27, 2018, from https://nctaf.org/wp-content/uploads/2012/01/NCTAF-Who-Will-Teach-Experience-Matters-2010-Report.pdf.

Davies, M., & Devlin, M. (2007). *Interdisciplinary higher education: Implications for teaching and learning.* Melbourne, Australia: Centre for the Study of Higher Education.

Duschl, R. A., & Bismack, A. S. (2016). *reconceptualizing stem education: the central role of practices.* New York: Routledge.

Duschl, R. A., Bismack, A. S., Greeno, J., & Gitomer, D. H. (2016). Coordinating preK–16 STEM education research and practices for advancing and refining reform agendas. In R. A. Duschl & A. S. Bismack (Eds.), *Reconceptualizing stem education: The central role of practices* (pp. 1–32). New York: Routledge.

English, L. D. (2016). STEM education K–12: Perspectives on integration. *International Journal of STEM Education, 3*(3), 1–8. DOI: 10.1186/s40594-016-0036-1

English, L. D., & Gainsburg, J. (2016). Problem solving in a twenty-first-century mathematics curriculum. In L. D. English & D. Kirshner (Eds.), *Handbook of international research in mathematics education* (3rd ed.; pp. 313–335). New York: Taylor & Francis.

Einstein, A. (1931). *Cosmic religion: With other opinions and aphorisms.* New York: Covici-Friede, Inc.

Felix, A., & Harris, J. (2010). A project-based, stem integrated: Alternative energy team challenge for teachers. *The Technology Teacher, 69*(5), 29–34.

Fioriello, P. (2010). Understanding the basics of STEM education. *Critical issues in K12 education* (online). Retrieved November 27, 2018, from http://drpfconsults.com/understanding-the-basics-of-stem-education/.

Golding, C. (2009). *Integrating the disciplines: Successful interdisciplinary subjects.* Melbourne, Australia: Center for the Study of Higher Education, University of Melbourne.

Hoachlander, G. (2014/2015). Integrating SET&M. *Educational Leadership* (December/January), 74–78.

Honey, M., Pearson, G., & Schweingruber, A. (2014). *STEM integration in K–12 education: status, prospects, and an agenda for research*. Washington, DC: National Academies Press.

Huber, M. T., & Hutchings, P. (2005). *Integrative learning: Mapping the terrain*. Washington, DC: Association of American Colleges and Universities.

Kalantzis, M., & Cope, B. (2014). Education is the new philosophy: To make a metadisciplinary claim for learning sciences. In A. D. Reid, P. E. Hart, & M. A. Peters (Eds.), *A companion to research in education* (pp. 101–115). New York: Springer-Verlag.

Kaufman, D., Moss, D., & Osborn, T. (Eds.). (2003). *Beyond the boundaries: A transdisciplinary approach to learning and teaching*. Westport, CN: Praeger.

King, H. (2011). Connecting in-school and out-of-school learning: An ISE research brief discussing tran's, the relationship between students' connections to out-of-school experiences and factors associated with science learning. Retrieved November 27, 2018, from http://www.relatingresearchtopractice.org/article/229.

Larson, R. C. (2013). STEM is for everyone. *WISE Newsletter*. August 23. Retrieved November 27, 2018, from http://www.wise-qatar.org/content/dr-larson-stem-everyone.

Ledbetter, M. L. S. (2012). Teacher preparation: One key to unlocking the gate to STEM literacy. *CBE—Life Sciences Education, 11*, 216–220.

Lederman, L. (1998). *ARISE: American renaissance in science education. Fermilab-TM-2051*. Batavia, IL: Fermi National Accelerator Lab.

Marginson, S., Tytler, R., Freeman, B., & Roberts, K. (2013). *STEM: Country comparisons*. Melbourne, Australia: Australian Council of Learned Academies

Milliken, D., & Adams, J. (2010). Recommendations for science, technology, engineering, and mathematics education. Report to Christine Gregoire, Governor, and the Washington State Legislature. Olympia, WA: Office of Superintendent of Public Instruction.

Moore, T. J., & Smith, K. A. (2014). Advancing the state of the art of STEM integration. *Journal of STEM Education, 15*(1), 5–10.

Morrison, J. S. (2006). *Attributes of STEM education: The students, the academy, the classroom*. TIES STEM Monograph Series. Baltimore, MD: Teaching Institute for Essential Science.

National Academy of Education. (2009). Education policy white paper: Science and mathematics education. J. Kilpatrick and H. Quin (Eds.). Washington DC: Author. Retrieved November 27, 2018, from https://files.eric.ed.gov/fulltext/ED531143.pdf.

National Research Council (NRC). (2011). *Successful K–12 STEM Education*. Washington, DC: The National Academies Press.

Partnership for 21st Century Skills. (2011). *Framework for 21st century learning*. Retrieved November 27, 2018, from http://www.p21.org/our-work/p21-framework.

President's Council of Advisors on Science and Technology (PCAST). (2011). Prepare and inspire: K–12 education in science, technology, engineering, and math (STEM) for America's future. Report to the president from the Whitehouse archives. Retrieved November 27, 2018, from https://obamawhitehouse.archives.gov/sites/default/files/microsites/ostp/pcast-stem-ed-final.pdf.

Read, T. (2013). *STEM can lead the way: Rethinking teacher preparation and policy.* San Francisco, CA: California STEM Learning Network.

Rennie, L., Wallace, J., & Venville, G. (2012). Exploring curriculum integration: Why integrate? In L. Rennie, G. Venville, & J. Wallace (Eds.), *Integrating science, technology, engineering, and mathematics* (pp. 1–11). New York: Routledge.

Sanders, M. E. (2008). STEM, STEM education, STEM mania. *The Technology Teacher, 68*(4), 20–26. Retrieved from https://vtechworks.lib.vt.edu/handle/10919/51616.

Sanders, M. E. (2012). Integrative STEM education as best practice. In H. Middleton (Ed.), *Explorations of best practice in technology, design, and engineering education*, vol. 2 (pp. 102–117). Gold Coast, AU: Griffith University.

Sanders, M. E. (2013). *Integrative STEM education: Retrospect/prospect.* Invited keynote paper presented at the EpiSTEME-5 Conference, Homi Bhabha Centre for Science Education, Mumbai, India, January 7–11.

STEM Task Force Report. (2014). *Innovate: A blueprint for science, technology, engineering, and mathematics in California public education.* Dublin, CA: Californians Dedicated to Education Foundation.

Stillman, J., & Anderson, L. (2014). Preparing the next generation of teacher educators. *Teachers College Record* (June 27). Retrieved November 30, 2018, from http://www.tcrecord.org (ID Number: 17581).

The NEA Foundation. (2012). Harnessing the potential of innovative STEM education programs: Stories of collaboration, connectedness and empowerment. Washington, DC: Author. Retrieved November 27, 2018, from https://www.neafoundation.org/wp-content/uploads/2017/08/nea_stemreport_final-5.pdf.

Traphagen, K., & Traill, S. (2014). *How cross-sector collaborations are advancing STEM learning.* Palo Alto, CA: Noyce Foundation.

Tsupros, N., Kohler, R., & Hallinen, J. (2009). *STEM education: A project to identify the missing components.* Intermediate Unit 1 for STEM Education. Pittsburgh, PA: Carnegie Mellon University.

Vasquez, J., Sneider, C., & Comer, M. (2013). *STEM lesson essentials, grades 3–8: Integrating science, technology, engineering, and mathematics.* Portsmouth, NH: Heinemann.

Virginia Tech. (n.d.). Integrative STEM education. Retrieved November 27, 2018, from https://liberalarts.vt.edu/departments-and-schools/school-of-education/academic-programs/integrative-stem-education.html.

Volk, T., & Bloom, J. W. (2007). The use of metapatterns for research into complex systems of teaching, learning, and schooling part II: Applications. *Complicity: An International Journal of Complexity and Education, 4*(1), 45–68.

Wells, J. G. (2013). Integrative STEM education at Virginia tech: Graduate preparation for tomorrow's leaders. *Technology and Engineering Teacher, 72*(5), 28–42.

Werth, A. (2003). Unity in diversity: The virtues of a metadisciplinary perspective in liberal arts education. *Journal of the National Collegiate Honors Council, 4*(2), 35–51.

Wilson, S. M. (2011). Effective STEM teacher preparation, induction, and professional development. Retrieved November 27, 2018, from http://sites.nationalacademies.org/cs/groups/dbassesite/documents/webpage/dbasse_072640.pdf.

Wilson, S. M. (2013). Recent development in STEM education to the qualities of teacher preparation program. Paper commissioned for the National Academy of Education. Funded by the National Science Foundation. Conference Paper. Workshop on Successful STEM Education in K–12 Schools. Washington, DC, May 10–11.

Part I

Interdisciplinary Thinking and Place-Based Practices in STEM

Interdisciplinary thinking in science, technology, engineering, and math (STEM) teacher preparation and practice requires a new level of understanding that transcends conventional approaches to teacher preparation. As Read (2012) explained, STEM thinking and pedagogy is "an interdisciplinary, applied approach that is coupled with real-world, problem-based learning" (p. 6).

Boix Mansilla, Miller, and Gardner (2000) proposed interdisciplinary understanding as "the capacity to integrate knowledge and modes of thinking in two or more disciplines or established areas of expertise to produce a cognitive advancement . . . ways that would have been impossible or unlikely through single disciplinary means" (p. 219).

Advocates of interdisciplinary teaching and learning in teacher preparation suggest that interdisciplinary approaches to coursework "promise a wide range of desirable educational outcomes for students" (Newell, 1994, p. 35). These outcomes include interdisciplinary perspectives, enhanced affective and cognitive abilities, increased understanding of complex problem solving, greater appreciation for ambiguity, and superior capacities for innovative thinking.

Spelt, Biemans, Tobi, Luning, and Mulder (2009) explained *interdisciplinary* in the context of teaching and learning in higher education as the "capacity to integrate knowledge of two or more disciplines to produce cognitive advancement in ways that would have been impossible or unlikely through single disciplinary means" (p. 365) through the application of complex cognitive skills.

Crampton, Ragusa, and Cavanagh (2012), in examining interdisciplinary thinking and learning, explained that it can be perceived as a radical restructuring of the whole learning process. This happens through constructing a pedagogical strategy that is experiential, place-based in nature, and a model of an integrative education based on advanced pedagogical and cross-disciplinary curricula design.

In STEM teacher preparation, this step forward in teacher preparation moves beyond traditional subject-based silo teaching (Czerniak, Weber, Sandmann, & Ahern, 1999). The notion of place-based learning and advanced problem-based learning pedagogies offers the opportunity for interdisciplinary thinking in a way as heretofore not experienced in more conventional teacher-preparation programs.

Engaging preservice teacher-preparation students in authentic tasks related to real-world, STEM-based problems enables experiential opportunities to directly apply interdisciplinary thinking and build necessary STEM skills and knowledge. Lattuca, Voigt, and Fath (2004) explained, "tasks associated with the problem replicate the data gathering, analysis, and problem solving that students expect to encounter in everyday life and work" (p. 32).

Stepping outside the traditional silos of knowledge associated with STEM and taking an interdisciplinary approach enables the teacher educator to situate preservice students in varying conditions that simulate unpredictable real-world environments and produces better learning outcomes, leading to interdisciplinary thinking and understanding necessary to new, creative pedagogies and learning (Halpern & Hakel, 2003).

Likewise, preservice students will gain experience that translates into classroom pedagogies when entering their classroom for the first time. Halpern and Hakel (2003) also noted that learning situated in place-based situations is enhanced when knowledge is acquired in one setting and applied in another. Interacting with challenging problems offers students opportunities to develop unique epistemological approaches (Holley, 2017). Importantly, interdisciplinary thinking is advanced when the learner is exposed to ill-structured problems that resemble the complex and dynamic nature of problems experienced in the real world (King & Kitchener, 1994).

Teacher preparation that engages the preservice teacher–student in interdisciplinary courses and place-based learning opportunities demonstrates opportunity for advancement of unconventional thinking and pedagogical strategies that more conventional teacher preparation does not (Ivanitskaya, Clark, Montgomery, & Primeau, 2002; Newell, 1994). The preservice teacher student situated in interdisciplinary learning experiences how to evaluate and synthesize new information and encounters unique opportunities to connect extant and emergent knowledge (Holley, 2017; Lattuca et al., 2004). Importantly, interdisciplinarity, as Weingart (2000) has pointed out, often carries with it positive connotations of progress, originality, and innovation that have currency in advancing an interdisciplinary STEM understanding of teacher preparation and practice.

Stepping beyond the traditional teacher-preparation program, one that is bound, contained, and even, restrictive in nature, is a necessary first step. The process of engaging interdisciplinarity in teacher preparation as a pedagogical strategy gives rise to opportunities for cross-disciplinary, collaborative inquiry and understanding of the next generation of STEM teachers.

REFERENCES

Boix Mansilla, V., Miller, W. C., & Gardner, H. (2000). On disciplinary lenses and interdisciplinary work. In S. Wineburg and P. Grossman (Eds.), *Interdisciplinary curriculum: Challenges of implementation* (pp. 17–38). New York, NY: Teachers College Press.

Cramptona, A., Ragusab, A., & Cavanagh, H. (2012). Cross-discipline investigation of the relationship between academic performance and online resource access by distance education students. *Research in Learning Technology, 20*, 14430. doi: 10.3402/rlt.v20i0/14430.

Czerniak, C. M., Weber, W. B., Sandmann, A., & Ahern, J. (1999). A literature review of science and mathematics integration. *School Science and Mathematics, 99*(8), 421–430.

Halpern, D., & Hakel, M. (2003). Applying the science of learning to the university and beyond: Teaching for long-term retention and transfer. *Change: The Magazine of Higher Learning, 35*(4), 36–41.

Holley, K. (2017). Interdisciplinary curriculum and learning in higher education. *Oxford Research Encyclopedia of Education.* oxfordre.com/education/view/10.1093/.../acrefore-9780190264093-e-138.

Ivanitskaya, L., Clark, D., Montgomery, G., & Primeau, R. (2002). Interdisciplinary learning: Process and outcomes. *Innovative Higher Education, 27*(2), 95–111.

King, P., & Kitchener, K. (1994). *Developing reflective judgment: Understanding and promoting intellectual growth and critical thinking in adolescents and adults.* San Francisco, CA: Jossey-Bass.

Lattuca, L., Voigt, L., & Fath, K. (2004). Does interdisciplinarity promote learning? Theoretical support and researchable questions. *The Review of Higher Education, 28*(1), 23–48.

Newell, W. (1994). Designing interdisciplinary courses. *New Directions for Teaching and Learning, 58*, 35–51.

Read, T. (2012). *Rethinking credentialing and teacher preparation: STEM can lead the way.* California STEM Learning Network. Tory Read Studio.

Spelt, E. J. H., Biemans, H. J. A., Tobi, H., Luning, P. A., & Mulder, M. (2009). Teaching and learning in interdisciplinary higher education: A systematic review. *Educational Psychology Review, 21*, 365–378. doi:10.1007/s10648-009-9113-z

Weingart, P. (2000). Interdisciplinarity: The paradoxical discourse. In P. Weingart and N. Stehr (Eds.), *Practising interdisciplinarity* (pp. 25–41). Toronto, Canada: University of Toronto Press.

Chapter 2

Toward an Eccentric Educational Ideal

The Demands for Interdisciplinary Thinking and Collaboration

Shawn Vecellio

Arguments have been advanced from a variety of authors that represent "demands" for an interdisciplinary approach to education in general and interdisciplinary thinking more specifically. These demands and their resolution will be cast in a series of three related "spheres of influence." These spheres are envisioned as beginning at the "smallest" (innermost) level of action, which is with K–12 classroom teachers and also scholars of the fields of study in traditional curricula (e.g., mathematicians, scientists).

Moving outward to broader considerations, the second sphere is the scholars and practitioners in the many subfields of education (e.g., educational philosophers, comparative educationists, "methods teachers," etc.). Finally, at the widest level is the sphere that includes scholars and practitioners from all fields of study and work, including artists, economists, those in sports medicine, and so forth.

This discussion begins by referencing several sources—some outside the field of education—that present demands on us inside the field. All referenced authors make arguments to the effect that an interdisciplinary approach in education is necessary, either by pointing directly to the need for it or alternatively to the dangers of neglecting it. After presenting the demands, the focus for the remainder of this chapter is on fleshing out the three spheres.

Each section opens with a brief recounting of my (the author's) experience at a conference on "Common Core State Standards: Implications for Language, Learning and Leadership" (October 2012). As educators have struggled to make sense of the demands that the new national-level standards make on all, there were numerous insights generated that spoke directly to the notion and need of interdisciplinary thinking in education.

The first subsection illustrates how classroom teachers might gather around certain thinking skills to form a version of thematic planning based on academic vocabulary. The second section explores what it might look like for professors in education-based fields to model collaborative work for K–12 teachers. The third section expands the scope of consideration to fields outside of education in the hope that theorists and practitioners in all areas of study and work can help those in education to formulate goals and solve problems.

Taken together, the three spheres of influence presented are meant to drive us toward an "eccentric" ideal of interdisciplinary thought and work in education as a countermeasure to the prevailing trend of specialization that seems to have us working in *con*centrically smaller and smaller circles. The chapter closes by drawing together a few conclusions and drawing out a few implications of the proposal.

CALLS FOR INTEGRATION FROM AFIELD

The most direct call for interdisciplinary learning comes from Palmer and Zajonc (2010) who argue for an "integrative form" of education. Although their recommendation is made for the higher education level, the rationale and examples they provide can certainly find parallels at the K–12 level.

Palmer and Zajonc argue for integrative education to teach the whole person and to prepare students in a sort of liberal education for the real, complex problems they will encounter in the work world. These sorts of demands appear throughout the paper in relation to the Common Core State Standards (CCSS) and to President Barack Obama's "Blueprint" for education/reform (see US Department of Education, 2010) with its mandate for all students to become "college and career ready."

Costa (2010) presents "silo thinking" as one of the most insidious roadblocks to modern problem solving in any area, including education. "Compartmentalized thinking and behaviors that prohibit the collaboration needed to address highly complex problems" (p. 131) are arguably part of what stand in the way of identifying appropriate goals and finding solutions to challenges in education. Costa's ideas figure into the proposal particularly in spheres two and three, where educationists are charged to work with others in related subfields and others outside education altogether.

Interdisciplinary thinking as a positive approach to problem solving and innovation is also supported by Csikszentmihalyi (1996) in his book *Creativity*. Having interviewed nearly one hundred "exceptional individuals" representing myriad fields of study and work, Csikszentmihalyi concludes that "creativity generally involves crossing the boundaries of domains" (p. 9). In place of disciplinary thinking, which is increasingly common in academic circles, a "holistic" or *adisciplinary* approach to creative thought and problem solving is offered as more amenable to addressing complex, real-world scenarios.

This argument in favor of cross-disciplinary work applies to the lesson-planning approach that will be illustrated (in sphere one) and the collaborative work educators need to do with others outside their own field (sphere three) to find redress for their biggest challenges. Indeed, some twenty years ago Csikszentmihalyi seems to have captured the present predicament and, fortunately, pointed toward a resolution:

> And what holds true for the sciences, the arts, and for the economy also applies to education. When school budgets tighten and test scores wobble, more and more schools opt for dispensing with frills—usually with the arts and extracurricular activities—to focus instead on the so-called basics. This would not be bad if the "three Rs" were taught in ways that encouraged originality and creative thinking: unfortunately, they rarely are. Students generally find the basic academic subjects threatening or dull; their chance of using their minds in creative ways comes from working on the student paper, the drama club, or the orchestra. So if the next generation is to face the future with zest and self-confidence, we must educate them to be original as well as competent. (1996, p. 12)

The account of the demands that the CCSS place on education figures in prominently here. There is an unprecedented movement toward standardization at the national level and so *how* curriculum and instruction is designed around these standards will be vital to the cognitive capabilities students develop.

Indeed, the continued focus on standards since No Child Left Behind (NCLB) has had a powerful impact on many areas of education. The increased expectation of subject-matter experts and "highly qualified teachers," for example, has led to more content-specific faculty and to greater training of teachers in specific subject areas. This has also affected hiring practices, such that middle schools are becoming more apt to hire secondary rather than primary teachers.

It is such political and economic pressures—referred collectively as "social dynamics"—pulling in one direction that I propose we must push against, that is, for students and teachers alike to think and work in more interdisciplinary ways. What follows shows how this push for "eccentricity" or interdisciplinary thinking and collaborative work within, across, and outside of education might look like.

TOWARD ECCENTRICITY:
Three Spheres of Thought and Work
Language and Thinking Skills—The Demands of National-Level Standards

The prevailing impression from the CCSS conference I attended was, frankly, confusion. But this confusion seemed grounded in hope: I left feeling that if indeed we are stumbling along during this time of significant change, we are at the very least fumbling *forward*. The CCSS represent an unprecedented reform/movement in US education, and these standards have far-reaching implications. What was heard over and over at this conference was an implicit argument around the *demands* that the CCSS make and many of these demands center on interdisciplinary modes of thought.

As national-level content standards, the CCSS along with the Next Generation Science Standards (NGSS) are a first-time venture and, as the conference emphasized, are beginning to take English learners more seriously than ever before. All three of these sets of standards, by design, entail an interdisciplinary mode of teaching and learning. Taken together, these two points suggest that both language skills and thinking skills are important considerations for how teachers design their instruction and for how teacher educators instruct about pedagogy.

One of the presentations at the conference that focused on the NGSS pointed directly to the interdisciplinary nature of national standards. In her presentation, Cheuk (2012) highlighted this dynamic by posing several questions: What are the language demands of the NGSS? What does *inquiry* look like across the disciplines? And, directing this question specifically to subject-area teachers, what is our shared language?

The various answers that Cheuk and others offered focused on thinking and literacy skills (e.g., citing, summarizing, paraphrasing; researching; understanding and expressing arguments; supporting and refuting claims and rebuttals). It is in these academic tasks that there is definite overlap in terms of expectations of thinking across multiple subject areas.

We can also recognize the notion of academic language/vocabulary at work. Here, *academic vocabulary* refers to thinking skills or processes that students are expected to engage in or master. They are the kinds of cognitive activities represented in Bloom's (cognitive) taxonomy and at the same time the terms (verbs) typically seen in content standards and their related educational objectives. This is the area explored further in the first sphere as one way we might think about moving from disciplinary to interdisciplinary thinking in the attempt to meet the demands of the CCSS.

Academic Vocabulary as Thinking Skills within and across the Disciplines

Some years ago, while teaching a lesson on thematic unit planning, I wanted to challenge my students to think about how we might replace "themes" with thinking skills. I put the issue as follows: What would happen if we tried to identify thought processes or disciplinary cognitive skills as the unifying factor for study?

Cognitive processes that are practiced across fields are in a sense generalizable or field independent, though of course the *content* on which the skills are applied remains subject *specific*. In that sense, there may be some nuance to a thinking skill that might be recognized as field *dependent*, but here we are seeking to identify modes of thought that can be addressed across multiple content areas.

Referring to the thematic units the class had sketched previously, the students were asked to review the content standards for the four core areas they had used and list the verbs from the objectives they had designed. Then they were to select one of the verbs and, envisioning that cognitive activity being used in each of the other three disciplines, compose a realistic objective based on that thinking skill for each of the remaining three areas. Students were offered the following example: Suppose the four verbs in our original standards were *list*, *describe*, *compute*, and *analyze* (for science, English, math, and history, respectively). Selecting *analyze* from the history area, the following objectives might be proposed for the other three areas:

- Science: students will be able to *analyze* the results of an experiment and suggest whether the conclusions provided make sense.
- English: students will be able to *analyze* a speech to determine whether certain fallacies have been used (e.g., appeals to authority).
- Math: students will be able to *analyze* information presented in various graphical forms to answer questions.

This example is straightforward because *analysis* is used in essentially every discipline. We struggled to find additional examples, however, so a decision was made to further pursue the inquiry. Among the thinking skills that cut across various disciplines considered were *interpret* and *explore*, but to illustrate the point, another skill was chosen.

Predicting is an activity often used in language arts when educators want to check children's comprehension of a story by asking them to predict what will happen next. Students in history might use prediction in a similar fashion, given certain contexts of war, for example. Further, in math, students use graphs, statistics, or probability to make predictions. And in a similar vein, in science, students predict what will happen in an experiment given certain conditions. Clearly, this was a thinking skill that had applications across all four core content areas.

At this point, it was decided to review the (California) state content standards to see if K–12 students are asked to engage in all these sorts of predictions. Although "predicting" was mentioned in each area (except history), there are other thought processes in each area that are *like* predicting.

Predicting is, of course, a fundamental reading comprehension skill used in English language arts. Conjecturing is a similar skill in mathematics, and hypothesizing is a similar skill in both the hard and social sciences. Each of these skills relates to a similar cognitive activity, namely, positing a claim about the unknown (often related to the future), which makes that thought process in some sense "interdisciplinary." However, performing each skill in context depends on field-dependent content, as is shown in the following descriptions:

- A student casts a prediction on what will happen in a story as a basis for demonstrating that he or she has understood the storyline thus far. The student thus needs to have comprehended the literature including the characters, plot, foreshadowing, and so forth.
- The student formulates a conjecture based on information provided about a mathematical problem or situation. To do so, he or she needs to have some understanding of the mathematical bases of the scenario, whether it relates to logic, geometry, statistics, and so on.
- The student generates a hypothesis in either the hard or social sciences based on an understanding of the key principles in question, whether it revolves around chemistry (e.g., proposing what will happen when elements are mixed) or economics (e.g., speculating on the effects of increased technology use on the labor market). To accomplish these, the student needs to understand something about compounds, reactions, and properties or how supply and demand, capital, and unemployment function.

What these examples provide is some direction toward interdisciplinary thought and work. The prediction case illustrates one specific example of how teachers and teacher educators can draw on the knowledge bases of the disciplines toward designing interdisciplinary lessons.

Additionally, the process of examining the content areas (whether by looking at standards or at what theorists and professionals in each discipline do) represents a method we can reiterate to locate additional cross-curricular examples. In effect, we can look at disciplinary thinking, research, and methods as tools of the trade for each subject area to identify cognitive processes that apply across multiple fields.

In other words, educators would be looking for skills that are "generalizable" or that *transfer*. With the skills at hand, both teachers and teacher educators could instruct their students on how these skills are used inter- and intradisciplinarily, which will help educators move toward meeting the demands of the CCSS.

THE "INNER CIRCLE":
COLLABORATION WITHIN THE FIELDS OF EDUCATION

"The only thing that's stopping me from working with my ELD [English Language Development] colleague down the hall is my own inertia." This was a comment from a science methods instructor during one of the conference presentations. It echoes the concern that Costa (2010) raised with regard to "silo thinking" and captures an important dynamic of the movement between sphere one and sphere two; if teacher educators are going to expect teachers to collaborate more across disciplinary boundaries, then it is incumbent on teacher educators to set an example.

The practice and modeling of collaboration across education fields in higher education will also help redress the problem of silo thinking and make progress toward solving the current educational problems and creating new ways of looking at educational aims.

Here it is important to relate the inner*most* circle of teachers and disciplinarians (i.e., English teachers and history teachers, mathematicians, and scientists), as exemplified in their future work in sphere one, to the next sphere of educators, which is all the higher-education faculty and researchers *within* the area of education studies. These practitioners and scholars can *model* what interdisciplinary collaboration should look like for K–12 teachers.

The foundations professor and the methods faculty, as well as the educational technology and the assessment instructors need to work together in an interdisciplinary manner. Teachers need to see and show how these subareas of understanding and applying education, teaching, and learning are themselves integrated. As has been suggested by scholars both inside and outside the field, we have gone too far in isolating these subfields and, in doing so, ourselves.

The separation of areas of study is represented in what seems a perennial predicament: integrated versus stand-alone courses. Do we set aside one course in inclusion, technology, diversity, assessment, or do we integrate these aspects in every course throughout the program? Teacher educators face this question every time a new course mandate is given.

And, in my experience (which is based on being a program reviewer for the state's credentialing agency), it seems that the vast majority most often elect to keep them segregated. (It would not necessarily be argued that this is simply an "intellectual silo" sort of decision. Practically speaking, the difficulty of rewriting a whole host of courses to integrate "health education," for instance, is certainly far costlier and demanding than simply adding in a distinct course on the topic.) In any case, this growing reality of increasing curriculum demands is one example of the sort of "social dynamics" relating to how silo thinking has been effected in our practice.

Against this backdrop, it is important to consider the conflicting messages teacher educators may be sending and receiving, specifically with regard to subject-specific knowledge compared with general pedagogical knowledge. Here another perennial debate should be entertained: the differences between the pedagogue—one who is well versed in the principles and methods of teaching and learning—and the subject matter expert—one who is well versed in a particular content area. To address this comparison, and to illustrate sphere two, it is appropriate to recount a personal education-based experience that sheds light on how a "specialist" mind-set can seep into work and thought and how it might be countered.

Differentiation of a Different Sort:
The Pedagogue, the SME, and Online Education

Setting the stage: One day, as the teacher goes to his classroom and tells his students, these would-be teachers, "You must be a facilitator. You must help the students bring their own prior knowledge to bear on the material at hand. You can't *give* them knowledge, but you can help them develop it for themselves." Then the teacher returns to his office after class and finds an e-mail inviting him to be the subject matter expert (SME) for some course that is being developed in an online format. "Yes, that's me, the SME," he thinks; "I'll take the job." This rub between the facilitator and the SME is, to the teacher's mind, a prime source of conflict for the modern educator.

The course that he was asked to participate in developing was in the area of "educational foundations." What was the employer looking for in a SME? Well, for one thing, they were *not* looking for *an instructor*. They would pull that person from their instructor pool, from a group who had experience in online teaching, though not necessarily anyone who had knowledge of the course content.

As the teacher later realized, part of the "virtue" of such courses is that they are designed to be foolproof or, as some refer to such "scripted" programs, "teacher-proof." So, as the SME, the teacher was supposed to put together a *curriculum* that essentially anyone could "manage." The "instructional" tasks would be rather limited to facilitating and evaluating student work.

As the SME, the teacher was expected to put together the content in a way that students could learn it. Here, he believed, is where the pedagogue—as opposed to the SME—enters in. For what the pedagogue knows above all else—and better than the SME—is to begin with the question: How is this subject best learned? The answer to that question will tell the pedagogue how the subject is best taught. And from there she can make decisions about the feasibility of teaching in ways that approximate the best way.

So this was the question for me: Given the online environment, what is the best way for students to learn about educational foundations? In other words, although the SME did help to develop several content objectives for the course—more properly the role of the SME—the main task was to figure out how best to get the students to those learning outcomes.

Part of what the teacher did was to develop "essential questions" that would help students get at the heart of the subject matter, the "big ideas." Granted, this takes a fair bit of subject matter knowledge. But at the same time, the teacher was developing activities for the students to engage in that would help them learn the subject. He knew how to design ways to help them access the material. He set the students up with exercises that would allow them to learn.

What is emphasized here is that the teacher "knew enough" to pose the essential questions, not simply *how* to pose questions about educational foundations because any SME could do that, but he knew that he *ought* to pose such questions. This, too, is what the pedagogue knows; she knows the principles behind theories such as "Understanding by Design" that deal with essential questions and big ideas (Wiggins & McTighe, 2005). She knows how to—and that she must—put these educational concepts and methods to work in the interest of student learning. The SME of a given content area does not *necessarily* have this knowledge or know-how.

To drive the point home, the teacher would later learn that his role in this case is often broken down into two. As it turns out, he was performing not only the SME role (according to the employer) but also the role of "course developer." This *differentiating of roles* is not uncommon for online courses (see, e.g., Neely & Tucker, 2010).

In courses that the same company subsequently designed, faculty were hired to play the role of SME, but they only needed to be present with the design team at the beginning of the project. After that point—after the *content* of the course had been identified with the help of the SME—the course developer would take over and determine how best to adapt that content to the online learning environment.

The teacher's experience in online-course development helped him to see more clearly the problem of the social dynamics that are effecting silo thinking in education circles. However, part of a solution to this problem is also contained in the scenario recounted: collaboration is key.

Educators in various fields need to work together both to create better educational experiences for our own students and for K–12 students as well. By working together—the curriculum specialists and the instructional designers, the pedagogues and the SMEs—we not only help to produce better educational experiences but we also model for teachers what interdisciplinary work and thought looks like and can produce.

THE OUTER SPHERE:
Setting Goals and Solving Problems

As one of the conference sessions concluded and a teacher exited the main ballroom, noticing a gathering in the atrium. These people wore different name badges than the educators had on, however, and as a teacher walked over to a billboard he realized that it was a stem-cell technology convention. He found it ironic that this group was right outside the door, as it were, and yet there was no intermingling between the camps: they had their own coffee and goodies set up separately. It was here that the boundaries of the silos were clear!

It made the educator wonder: What would these people say if they attended the educator conference sessions? What ideas might they contribute to help resolve the problems raised? What suggestions might they make for how students are educated? And, finally, were any of these folks consulted when the NGSS were created?

These are the sorts of questions we must confront honestly if we take seriously the call to interdisciplinary work in and around education. This is the third sphere of influence that must be addressed in two ways or for two reasons. First, we in education must reach out to others in other fields—*all* other fields—to help identify what the modern aims of education ought to be.

Stakeholders and personnel from all sorts of professions ought to be consulted as we seek to identify what students should know and be able to do. They should be consulted as well regarding our aims of education more broadly speaking; that is, as we seek to determine what we are preparing students for.

Second, and as a correlate to this first point, we in education ought to consult more with others in outside fields to help get new perspectives on how to address our challenges. This is what the authors previously cited in this chapter advocate when they speak of working collaboratively across disciplines to address complex, systemic, and seemingly intractable problems.

This is a third sphere of interdisciplinary work, which includes educators of all sorts interacting with scholars and researchers as well as professionals and practitioners in every field of study and across every line of work. To make this argument, it is appropriate to draw on another mandate—a legislative one—that also makes demands on us in terms of interdisciplinary education.

From Work to School: Developing a Notion of Authentic Curriculum and Instruction

During the "superintendents' panel" at the conference, it was suggested that the goal of "college and career readiness" is itself a mandate for K–12 *and* higher education to involve business leaders, economists, and others in their decision making and planning processes. At all levels of education, we need to involve those who cannot only help us to identify education goals but also help us address our problems from a more rounded, realistic perspective.

The aim to have all high school graduates "college and career ready" comes from President Obama's "Blueprint." As the superintendents referenced this goal, I was reminded of an article by Rose arguing for a reintegration of academic and technical-vocational studies. "[D]eeply rooted in American educational history is the sharp distinction between academic and vocational study" (Rose 2011). This made me wonder whether the intent is really to make all students both college *and* career ready or just to make each student college *or* career ready.

If students are to be prepared for some range of careers as well as for college, then we will have to understand what those careers and colleges require of them. Surely those skills are going to be some of the ones that cut across disciplines, as fields of study approximate fields of work.

Here, again, is the demand: educationists must know what skills need to be taught, and we can learn that from talking to professionals outside our own subject area of expertise. This recapturing of vocational- or career-based knowledge and skills seems justified for the same reasons that pedagogies of project- and problem-based learning are: because they are drawn from the real world, where the tasks and issues are complex and messy (i.e., still integrated or adisciplinary).

If we take this demand seriously, what it leads us toward is the need for a notion of "authentic curriculum and instruction" to complement *authentic assessment*. And strides are already being made along related lines in terms of "Smarter Balanced Assessments" and "linked learning." What is suggested is that we extend these efforts by consulting more with professionals and practitioners to help us identify realistic scenarios for students to use as learning situations and real problems to replace the typical textbook exercises.

What this sort of approach might lead to is the development of more integrated coursework (contrary to what was noted previously about how we tend to develop isolated courses). Traditional courses in math and English using a problem-based learning approach would be a step in the right direction, but a course in problem solving itself may go even further toward meeting the demand.

The problems in such a course would be integrated, realistic if not real, and teachers would have to be versed in virtually every field. But this is what we already expect of primary teachers, and it is also in keeping with the demand most often raised at the CCSS conference: cross-curricular teaching is now everyone's responsibility. English teachers are now expected to address science content and math teachers are supposed to develop writing skills, and so on.

What this brings us back to is that "social dynamic" that we seem to be immersed in, which is pushing us toward greater specialization, disciplinary learning, and subject-matter expertise. And it is this trend toward the "concentric"—smaller and smaller circles of knowledge and skill—that I am ultimately suggesting we need to reverse. That is why advocating for an "eccentric" form of thinking as an educational ideal is important.

We need to work across disciplines to solve our problems, and we need to have students solving problems that cross disciplines as well. We need to increase our spheres of consideration, to set our goals interdisciplinarily, and to solve our problems collaboratively. In short, we need to work closer and think broader.

CONCLUSIONS

The take-home message received from the CCSS conference was that teaching the various content areas is a shared responsibility. The science teacher is also a language teacher and the history teacher must include math in those lessons. The CCSS demand this kind of interdisciplinary work by teachers. This is sphere one. The "language demands" are there, in every discipline, but so are the "disciplinary" demands in all the language-based tasks.

Here is a mandate for greater interdisciplinary understanding and collaboration than we have ever before seen in education. And the demands apply as much to student learning as they do to teacher instruction. Interdisciplinary thinking is necessary for both.

Academic vocabulary provides one source for us to look for answers to the kind of interdisciplinary thinking (skills) that we might want to pursue.

Once identified, these cross-disciplinary thinking skills can be something we focus on in teacher education as well. The cognitive skills identified as cutting across subject matters could become some of what we as teacher educators teach to our students as teacher candidates.

In addition to identifying cognitive *activities* that lend themselves to an interdisciplinary approach, we could also look for *concepts* that apply across disciplines, which would be somewhat different from the "themes" normally associated with such lesson planning. A few examples worth pursuing might be *data*, *evidence*, *pattern*, and *change* because each of these applies across subject areas.

Furthermore, once we have either a concept or skill in mind, we could look for its counterpart. For instance, given that we are dealing with *patterns* in history, we could then ask what we do with them. One answer is that we *identify* them. So identifying might be a thinking skill that cuts across subjects. Given the task of *interpreting*, we can ask what we interpret in a certain field. In math, for instance, we interpret *data*. This line of inquiry could thus help us identify additional ideas for interdisciplinary thought.

The implications of the demands outlined also affect the work of teacher educators. Interdisciplinary teaching and learning necessitate a focus on alternative pedagogies, those that arguably have not been used to their full potential, especially in the years following the wave of state-based content standards and standardized tests that grew out of NCLB. Although these seemed to leave less and less room for multidisciplinary modes of thinking and teaching, we are now in a position to concentrate on approaches that do include complex problems and real-world scenarios such as problem- and project-based learning.

The implication that teacher educators need to begin to prepare teachers more in the ways of such alternative pedagogies in turn has implications for policy makers, standards writers, and curriculum designers at the district, state, and national levels and for professional development by administrators at the school level. Because the national standards are new, most sets of *professional* standards probably do not include these considerations.

Although bodies such as state departments of education and credentialing agencies have historically sought to ensure that professional standards were in alignment with *content* standards, the professional standards will now have to be reconfigured to account for new approaches to interdisciplinary teaching and learning. This will also impact *program* standards, how teacher education programs are structured, and what (and how) teacher educators are expected to teach.

Fortunately, some of these concerns are currently being addressed. At one of the conference presentations, the English Language Proficiency Development Framework (Council of Chief State School Officers, 2012) was introduced.

Although it has been suggested that we reach out across disciplinary boundaries to both scholars and practitioners of all areas to identify problems and scenarios worth working on, given where we stand with the existing CCSS and NGSS, we could start with these instead and look for overlap.

As the standards get revised over time, future research should include both scholars and practitioners in efforts to identify key content in their areas and then working collaboratively to design cross-disciplinary lessons. This, sphere three, is the basis for developing a rich notion of authentic curriculum and instruction to complement authentic assessment.

The second sphere identified, which entails teacher educators working collaboratively with scholars across all education-related subfields, is probably the place to begin *because* this is the point of modeling for K–12 teachers and others outside our fields. We in education must take the lead or at least join in where others have already begun.

Here, an example provided by Palmer and Zajonc (2010) is important to consider. We in higher education must set the tone and the precedent for K–12 teachers. We have to teach them what it means to work collaboratively and the value of interdisciplinary study and learning by addressing multifaceted, systemic problems. And we can do this best by doing it ourselves. We have all the mandates we need that support the utility and propriety of this kind of work. We need not wait for another one to tell us how to do it or that we can.

REFERENCES

Cheuk, T. (2012). Common Core state standards: Implications for language, learning, and leadership. Presented at Project CORE: San Diego State University College of Education and California Department of Education, San Diego, CA.

Costa, R. (2010). *The watchman's rattle: Thinking our way out of extinction.* Philadelphia, PA: Vanguard Press.

Council of Chief State School Officers (CCSSO). (2012). *Framework for English language proficiency development standards corresponding to the Common Core State standards and the next generation science standards.* Washington, DC: Author.

Csikszentmihalyi, M. (1996). *Creativity: Flow and the psychology of discovery and invention.* New York, NY: HarperCollins.

Neely, P., & Tucker, P. (2010). Unbundling faculty roles in online distance education programs. *The International Review of Research in Open and Distance Learning, 11*(2). Retrieved November 27, 2018, from http://www.irrodl.org/index.php/irrodl/article/view/798/1554.

Palmer, P., & Zajonc, A. (2010). *The heart of higher education: A call to renewal.* San Francisco, CA: Jossey-Bass.

Rose, M. (2011). Making sparks fly: How occupational education can lead to a love of learning for its own sake. *The American Scholar, 8*(3), 35–43. Retrieved November 27, 2018, from http://theamericanscholar.org/making-sparks-fly/.

US Department of Education. (2010). *A blueprint for reform: The reauthorization of the elementary and secondary education act*. Washington, DC: Author. Retrieved November 27, 2018, from http://www2.ed.gov/policy/elsec/leg/blueprint/blueprint.pdf.

Wiggins, G., & McTighe, J. (2005). *Understanding by design* (2nd ed.). Alexandria, VA: Association for Supervision and Curriculum Development.

Chapter 3

Looking Deeper through the STEM Lens

Exploring the Intersection between Content and Context to Optimize STEM Learning

Louis S. Nadelson and Anne L. Seifert

Science, technology, engineering, and math (STEM) have become linked through association and overlap within research and development that are connected to solving complex problems, global competitiveness, and growing economic prosperity (Carnevale, Smith, & Melton, 2011). Simultaneously, science, technology, engineering, and mathematics remain as discrete topics in traditional education systems that are frequently taught using traditional instructional approaches (Buck, Bretz, & Towns, 2008).

MULTIPLE PERSPECTIVES:
Defining STEM

The potential for a wide range of perspectives of STEM has led us to define STEM on a continuum (Nadelson, Seifert, & Chang, 2013; figure 3.1). Our definition of STEM is inclusive and could bring clarity to each unique perspective or configuration of STEM that people refer to in their discussions of STEM.

We consider the definition of STEM through two lenses. The first lens is the configurations of STEM with regard to the extent that STEM disciplines are amalgamated or isolated. The second lens is the common ways people view teaching and learning associated with various configurations of STEM. We maintain that there is a high level of correlation between different configurations of STEM and teaching and learning of STEM.

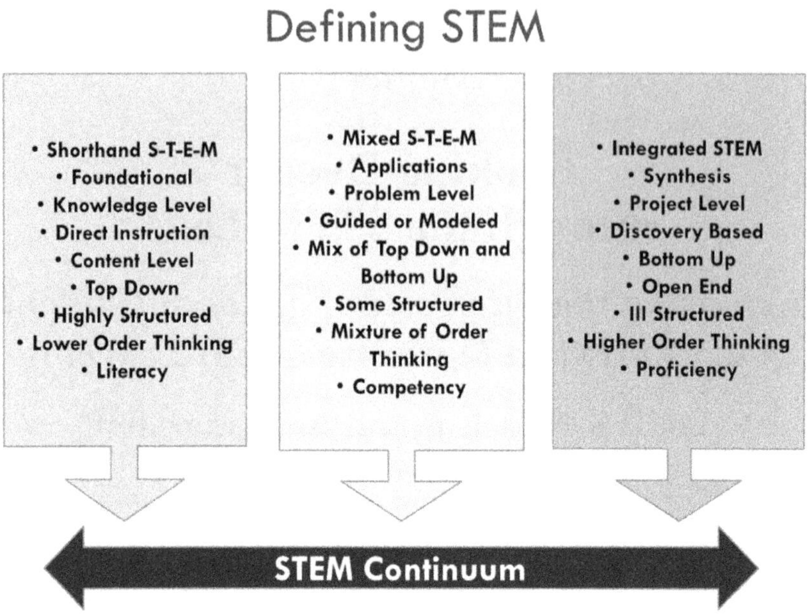

Defining STEM

- Shorthand S-T-E-M
- Foundational
- Knowledge Level
- Direct Instruction
- Content Level
- Top Down
- Highly Structured
- Lower Order Thinking
- Literacy

- Mixed S-T-E-M
- Applications
- Problem Level
- Guided or Modeled
- Mix of Top Down and Bottom Up
- Some Structured
- Mixture of Order Thinking
- Competency

- Integrated STEM
- Synthesis
- Project Level
- Discovery Based
- Bottom Up
- Open End
- Ill Structured
- Higher Order Thinking
- Proficiency

STEM Continuum

Figure 3.1 Defining STEM on a continuum. *Source*: author created.

Therefore, there is justification for considering multiple aspects of STEM research and education when defining STEM, particularly in the context of education. We have developed a continuum to include the range of possibilities and configurations of STEM as a result of these multiple possible perspectives of STEM.

At one end of the continuum, STEM is defined as anything that has an emphasis related to science, technology, engineering, or mathematics. This end of the continuum is commonly found in schools, with science, technology, engineering, and mathematics typically taught as discrete subjects and where STEM disciplines do not overlap. Also consistent with traditional approaches to education, the interaction with STEM at this end of the continuum is top down, with knowledge distributed by teachers to students. The engagement with STEM is at the fundamental or foundational knowledge level and, therefore, requires lower-order thinking and learning skills. We define this end of the continuum as the *STEM knowledge and literacy level*.

As we move toward the middle of the STEM continuum, we maintain there are increasing combinations of STEM disciplines. This area of the spectrum is exemplified by combining knowledge from two or more domains for success with STEM, such as with calculus-based physics.

Another example is computer science, which involves the combination of technology and mathematics. In this area of the STEM continuum, the focus is on problems and may involve a combination of top-down and bottom-up learning, exemplified by a combination of direct instruction and student-centered inquiry. Similarly, we have observed a mixture of lower- and higher-order thinking skills in this region of the continuum. Operating within this region requires a *STEM competency level of understanding and ability*.

At the other end of the continuum, STEM is fully integrated, and the focus is no longer on the content, but on the problem or project. At this end of the continuum, STEM is better represented as an *intellectual toolbox* from which individuals draw tools of STEM knowledge and procedures to solve problems, create products, and develop solutions.

Societal needs for STEM motivate engagement at this end of the continuum because individuals or groups draw on STEM knowledge and processes to address ill-structured complex situations that have no apparent specific solutions. At this end of the continuum, we find STEM professionals working on large-scale projects related to energy, food, water, manufacturing, transportation, and health care. Individuals working on this end of the STEM continuum are at the *proficiency level*.

We do not advocate that all STEM that takes place in schools shift to the integrated end of the STEM continuum; rather, we maintain that students should be exposed to a wide variety of STEM configurations. Fundamental STEM knowledge needs to be addressed before more complex applications.

However, we also maintain that educators need to be fluid in their movement across the STEM continuum, providing students with projects or problems that require them to engage their STEM-intellectual toolbox, particularly to address the practices of the Common Core State Standards-Math (CCSS-M) and the Next Generation Science Standards (NGSS) (Common Core State Standards Initiative, 2010; NGSS Lead States, 2013).

Offering a curriculum in which student engagement with STEM moves across the STEM continuum is critical to prepare students for the STEM workforce and to develop deeper understanding of STEM content, context, and processes. Further, the integration STEM process is more effective and efficient for creating opportunities for students to engage in the multiple practices from CCSS-M and the NGSS. Conversely, staying in the siloed end of the continuum is likely to require only application of a narrow range of the practices, if practices are addressed at all.

MULTIPLE VIEWS OF STEM

How people view STEM and the way that they use STEM depends on the situations of environments in which they interact with STEM (figure 3.2; Nadelson & Seifert, 2014). For example, it is common in schools for STEM to be typically focused on learning STEM content for the purpose of learning more STEM content. A student may learn algebra to be able to solve problems in trigonometry.

Thus, the traditional educational view of STEM is content driven, with standards, curriculum, and teacher knowledge heavily influencing the forms of STEM teachers use to engage their students and how students interact with specific STEM content. As a result, STEM in schools is typified by implementing isolated disciplines, with little overlap among STEM content. Because of this focus on the process of learning STEM to learn more STEM, it reduces the likelihood of being able to effectively address practices and expectations of the CCSS-M and the NGSS.

In contrast to schools, the view on STEM in business and industry is driven by context rather than content. Through the "business and industry" lens, STEM is envisioned not as a canon of knowledge to be acquired to learn more STEM, but as a toolbox of knowledge for solving complex problems and developing unique solutions. For example, a wide range of STEM content and processes may be used to construct next-generation computers or develop disease-resistant crops. Thus, it is the context of the problems or knowledge required for developing solutions that determines which elements of STEM are focused on.

Unlike what is typically encountered in education, the context for STEM in business and industry shifts and evolves rapidly, requiring a broad and agile view of STEM that is readily influenced by new knowledge and new possibilities and responsive to new needs, opportunities, and developments. STEM in business and industry is seamlessly integrated, driven by context of

Education
- Content for more content
- Content driven

Workplace
- Content for solving problems
- Context driven

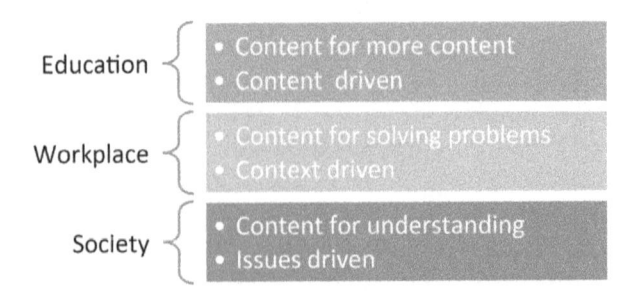

Society
- Content for understanding
- Issues driven

Figure 3.2 Motivation and use of STEM in schools, industry, and society.
Source: author created.

problems and desire for solutions rather than content. As a result of the application of STEM in these conditions, practices of the NGSS and CCSS-M are addressed without concerted effort due to the context because these practices are essential components for the effective implementations of problem-based, solution-driven contextualized STEM.

A third possible view of STEM is through the eyes of societal lens in which STEM is viewed as critical to understanding complex issues and perhaps developing explanations and exposing potential ramifications of STEM-related issues to individuals and the greater society (see figure 3.2). It is through STEM that people bring meaning to and solutions for issues such as those that impact the health and welfare of society. For example, STEM is needed to accurately detail the pros and cons of genetically modified foods, or predict the time, location, and impact of the next major earthquake. In this context, STEM is multidisciplinary and pragmatic, with the focus shifting depending on the current needs and events in society.

We maintain that there is merit to all these views of STEM and advocate for STEM in education to be more flexible, adopting the different perspectives of STEM, and using these perspectives to effectively teach students STEM. Implementation of curriculum and instruction from various perspectives increases the likelihood of assuring student workforce readiness and preparing them to engage in discussions and decisions on STEM-related societal issues.

Conversely, traditional STEM curriculum in school is unlikely to sufficiently address the STEM practices of the NGSS and CCSS-M because these require a broader view of STEM (e.g., Mayes & Koballa, 2012). Further, the needs of the workplace and society suggest that there is a need to shift the view of STEM in K–12 education to include a more integrated applied perspective.

INCREASING POWER:
Transdisciplinary Contexts for Interdisciplinary Habits of Mind

Major STEM issues of society and STEM challenges of business and industry are typically complex and are transdisciplinary by necessity (Hirsch Hadorn et al., 2008). Developments such as genetically modified foods, adequate supply and distribution of potable water, vaccines, energy generation and use, and solid waste disposal require knowledge of multiple areas of chemistry, physics, biology, biomedical engineering, civil engineering, mechanical engineering, materials sciences, mathematics, computer hardware and software, and geology.

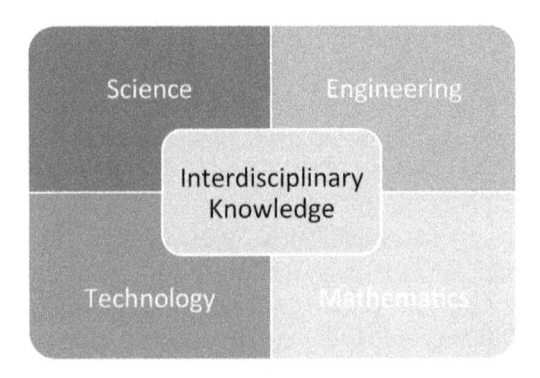

Figure 3.3 Intersection of science, technology, engineering, and mathematics knowledge leads to interdisciplinary knowledge. *Source*: author created.

Yet, to find solutions to these developments or comprehend them for decision making requires the associated STEM knowledge to be seamlessly integrated and overlapping (or transitioning and transferring) in a manner that is focused not on content but on the application of the knowledge in the context of the development (Nadelson, Seifert, Moll, & Coats, 2012). It is where these disciplines overlap that the creative and viable solutions are found for these complex problems (figure 3.3). Overlap of multiple disciplines is also needed to understand and make informed decisions on complex issues in society.

The integration of disciplines is common outside of traditional school learning environments. For example, it is assumed that professionals in chemical engineering have a background in, and will apply knowledge from, multiple disciplines such as mathematics, computing, materials, circuits, chemistry, physics, engineering, geology, biology, and other areas.

A significant challenge with transdisciplinary work is the expectation that professionals will be able to select the appropriate discipline-based knowledge and effectively apply that knowledge toward the interdisciplinary context. The barriers are founded in both the nature of learning and in the mind, conditions that limit our ability to readily transfer knowledge where the circumstances are not consistent with those in which the learning took place (Bransford, Brown, & Cocking, 1999).

However, transfer of knowledge can be facilitated by exposing students to a wide range of opportunities to apply their knowledge (Haskell, 2001), which encompasses the practices of the NGSS and CCSS-M. Thus, there is justification for providing students with a curriculum in which they have multiple chances to apply their learning in a wide range of contexts.

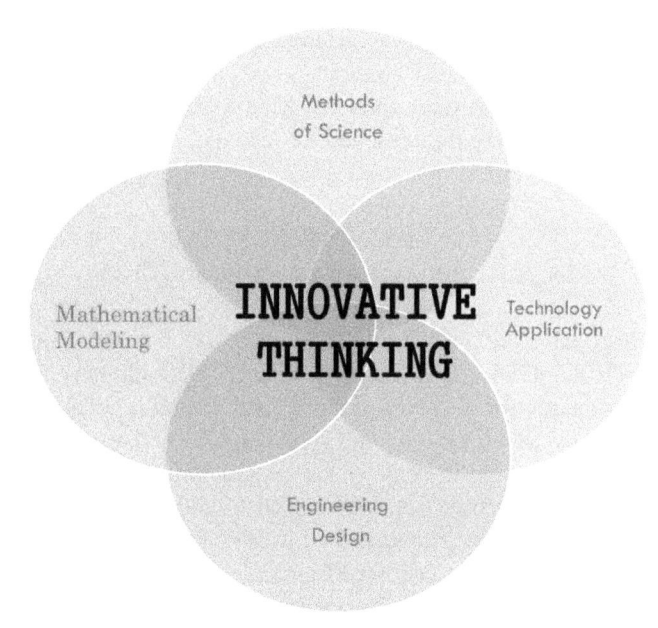

Figure 3.4 The overlap of STEM practices leads to innovative thinking.
Source: author created.

Further, when students are immersed in contexts in which the application of knowledge is transdisciplinary, they can experience transfer of knowledge from several disciplines toward common problems, which increases efficiency in teaching and facilitates student development of an interdisciplinary perspective and overlap of NGSS and CCSS-M practices.

In addition to creating opportunities to combine knowledge from multiple disciplines, transdisciplinary contexts also afford opportunities to combine the practices of the STEM disciplines. Transdisciplinary context requires the application of scientific practices, the modeling of mathematics, the design of engineering, and the application of technology.

We argue that it is at the intersection of these practices where we find *innovative thinking* (figure 3.4). Transdisciplinary work requires new ways of thinking, which require *habits of mind* that seek solutions and ideas using a range of practices that cross and combine disciplines in processes that overlap considerably with the NGSS and CCSS-M practices (Nadelson, Seifert, & Hettinger, 2012).

By engaging our students in integrated STEM learning activities that foster the use of a range of STEM practices, educators can help them develop habits of mind that seek solutions using different perspectives. Integrated STEM learning contexts also provide students with opportunities to gain deeper understanding of STEM through the lens in the workplace combined with the power of transdisciplinary thinking and knowledge.

NEW LENSES FOR STEM:
Integration and Application of STEM

We have observed a shift in the lenses through which K–12 educators have examined STEM. NGSS, CCSS-M, the CSTA K–12 Computer Science Standards, and Standards for K–12 Engineering Education have all provided us with new lenses by which we look at STEM teaching and learning. Although, there may be new content in some of these standards, we postulate that the real power of the standards is promoting instruction that supports student development of the STEM practices.

The practices of NGSS and CCSS-M indicate that STEM should be taught within an applied transdisciplinary manner that is project based, student centered, and involves authentic contexts for learning (figure 3.5).

Upon examination of the practices of CCSS-M and NGSS it becomes apparent that there is substantial overlap. The overlap of these practices indicates that there are many similarities to teaching and learning mathematics, science, and engineering, which provides support for using an integrated STEM approach to teach the subjects both independently and combined.

For example, when teaching linear equations in mathematics, there is great benefit to using contexts from science and engineering to engage students in data collection, analysis, modeling, and interpretation activities that lead to a deeper understanding of linear relationships. Further, increased overlap in the practices of mathematics, science, and engineering become more relevant, purposeful, and efficient for the students while fostering student engagement in and mastery of the practices.

GREATER MAGNITUDE:
Content with Context

As we discussed previously, it is common in schools for the context for teaching STEM content to be for learning more STEM content (see figure 3.2). However, STEM content outside of school relies on solving problems in a wide range of contexts. A significant problem with conventional STEM-content teaching is that this approach is not aligned with the context in which students encounter STEM outside of school in society and the workplace and, therefore, such teaching may not prepare them well (Nadelson & Seifert, 2014).

Power of Practices

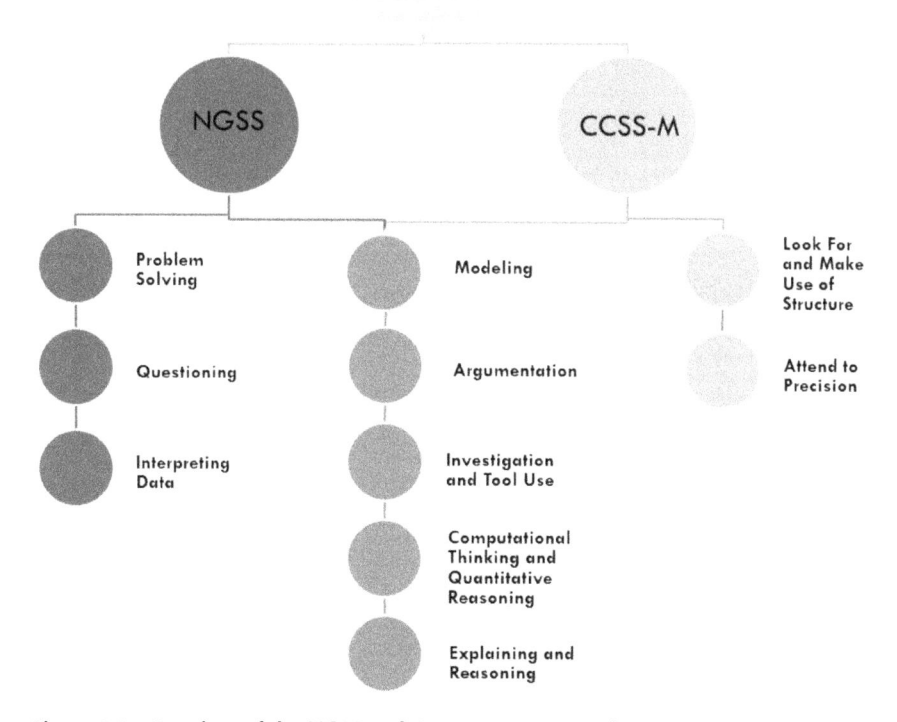

Figure 3.5 Practices of the NGSS and CCSS-M. *Source*: author created.

NGSS: Problem Solving, Questioning, Interpreting Data, Modeling, Argumentation, Investigation and Tool Use, Computational Thinking and Quantitative Reasoning, Explaining and Reasoning

CCSS-M: Look For and Make Use of Structure, Attend to Precision

We cannot expect student content knowledge to be readily and effectively transferred to content application, particularly in novel situations. Therefore, we argue that if we want students to effectively move about the STEM spectrum and engage in a variety of contexts, then they need to experience learning STEM content in context more aligned with society and workplace needs. Further, teaching STEM content in authentic contexts is aligned with and facilitates NGSS and CCSS-M practices. Thus, creating situations that address workplace and society contexts is likely to promote student engagement in the NGSS and CCSS-M practices.

Teaching STEM content with contexts that are authentic and applied at the integrated end of the STEM spectrum (see figure 3.1) will provide students and teachers with answers to the question: Where will I ever use this? Research shows that when students apply their knowledge to authentic contexts they develop deeper understanding of the content, are more motivated to learn, are more likely to retain the concepts, and have increased abilities to transfer the content to other contexts (Bransford, Brown, & Cocking, 1999).

Thus, teaching using an integrated STEM approach provides a means of learning the concepts in context that will deepen students' understanding of the content and increase their understanding of how the content can be applied to solve more complex and challenging problems of workplace and society.

IMAGE OF OPTIMIZATION:
The Model

We contend that there is an optimal alignment between levels of student content knowledge and the structure of the context that could be used to teach the STEM content (figure 3.6). In our model, we promote an alignment between the extent of STEM content knowledge and the complexity of the context used to engage students in STEM learning. For example, if students are being introduced to a concept for the first time and have low levels of STEM knowledge, they should be engaged in activities such as identifying or classifying situations related to targeted STEM content.

In contrast, if students have high levels of content knowledge then teachers should create opportunities for their students to apply their knowledge toward innovation. For example, students with a high knowledge of chemistry may be engaged to develop ideas and processes for recycling water bottles that

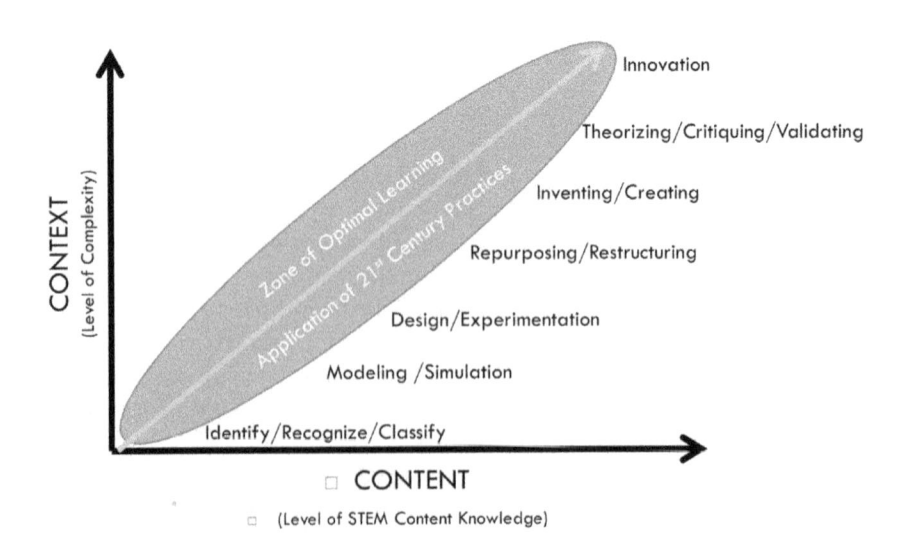

Figure 3.6 Alignment between level of content knowledge and level of complexity of learning context. *Source*: author created.

minimize impact on environment while maximizing application of knowledge and working toward a solution that advances society.

We maintain that the alignment between content and context is critical. If students with low levels of content knowledge are presented with an assignment that is perceived as a highly complex context, students are likely to experience frustration and disengage from learning. Similarly, if students with a high level of content knowledge are given an assignment that is low in complexity, students are likely to finish the task rapidly, become bored, and gain little or nothing from the assignment. Thus, alignment between levels of content knowledge and level of complexity of the context needs to be appropriate such that they meet and perform in the "zone of optimal learning."

A teacher seeking to effectively immerse students in the zone of optimal learning and attend to the NGSS and CCSS-M practices will need to consider the learning capacity of students, the content knowledge of students, meaningful applications of STEM, student learning objectives, and alignment with opportunities to engage students in the practices.

A teacher's ability to engage students in the proper context-content alignment is likely to take some experimenting, with redesign taking place with new groups of students where new ideas develop, new resources become available, students gain content and contextual knowledge, and the teacher becomes more effective at teaching in manners that engage students in a wide range of contexts aligned to their development and application of content knowledge.

FOCUS AND IDENTIFY:
Applications and Examples for Integration

Approaching the teaching of the NGSS and CCSS-M practices and associated STEM content using authentic contexts is likely to be most effectively achieved taking an integrated STEM approach. The contexts that are available using an integrated STEM approach are likely to be broad in scope and rich in opportunities. Consider the common design activity in which students develop a container to hold an egg such that when dropped from a height and hits the ground the shell of the contained egg does not crack. The "egg-drop" activity is rich in both the STEM content that can be addressed as well and the level of complexity on which the assignment might be structured.

To determine both the content and context of project-based assignments such as the egg-drop activity, we have developed a STEM Activity Decomposition Tool (Nadelson, Seifert, & Hettinger, 2012) by which educators can examine such assignments to determine the range of potential STEM content that might be addressed (figure 3.7). We demonstrate the use of the STEM Activity Decomposition Tool using the egg-drop activity as a context, considering the possible STEM concepts or content addressed within

Top diagram (template)

Science — Concepts/Content

Technology — Concepts/Content

Contextual Concept Based STEM Activity

Concepts/Content

Concepts/Content

Engineering

Math

Bottom diagram (Egg Drop)

Science
- Force
- Motion – Velocity & Acceleration
- Distance
- Momentum
- Gravity
- Projectiles
- Energy Transfer
- PE KE
- Data collection
- Measurement
- Biology of Eggs

Technology
- Paper
- Plastic
- Bubble wrap
- Rubber
- Scissors
- Ladder

Integrated STEM

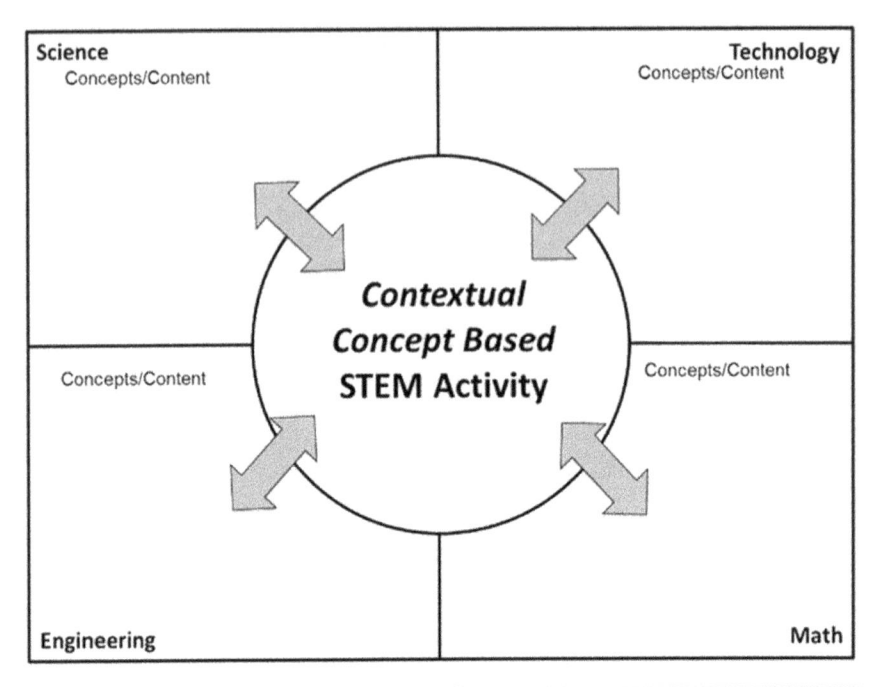

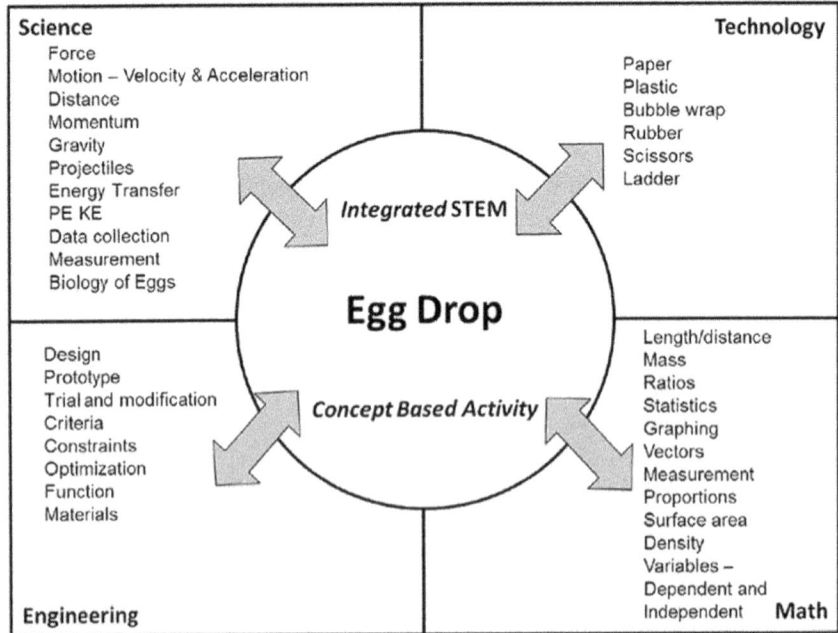

Egg Drop

Concept Based Activity

Engineering
- Design
- Prototype
- Trial and modification
- Criteria
- Constraints
- Optimization
- Function
- Materials

Math
- Length/distance
- Mass
- Ratios
- Statistics
- Graphing
- Vectors
- Measurement
- Proportions
- Surface area
- Density
- Variables – Dependent and Independent

Figure 3.7 STEM Activity Decomposition Tool template and with data for the egg-drop activity. *Source*: author created.

each of the four STEM domains. We have identified several potential topics from each of the four STEM domains that could be addressed with the egg drop project.

Our consideration resulted in more than thirty concepts (as shown in figure 3.7) that could be addressed using this single activity. However, it is likely that the number of concepts and diversity of content that could be addressed may be more extensive depending on the structure of the assignment, student content knowledge, and available resources. Our example illustrates how a relatively simple activity can be used to teach a wide range of STEM concepts and content in context. Further, active engagement in the process is likely to facilitate integration of multiple CCSS-M and NGSS practices.

CONCLUSIONS

We have presented a case for teaching STEM content and concepts in context. Our justification is increased motivation, engagement, retention, and deeper processing that takes place when students learn in context, as well as greater contextual alignment with STEM engagement outside of schools. In figure 3.8, we present how the multiple lenses come together to create

Why Content in Context?

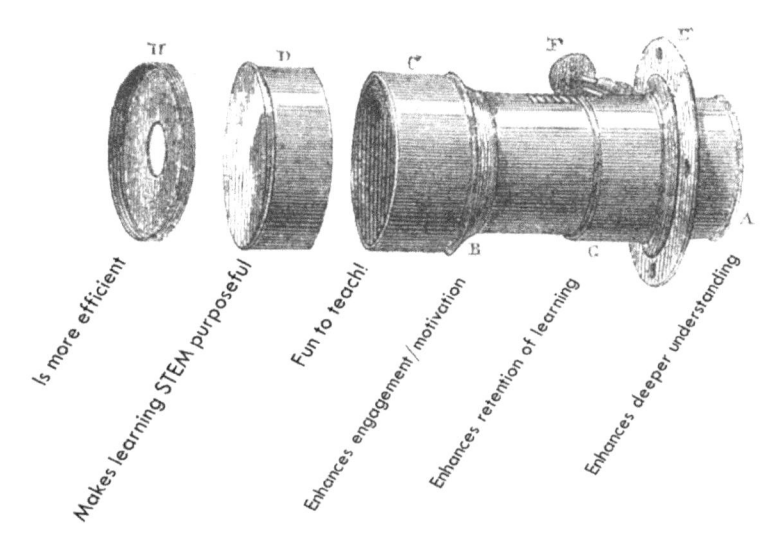

- Is more efficient
- Makes learning STEM purposeful
- Fun to teach!
- Enhances engagement/motivation
- Enhances retention of learning
- Enhances deeper understanding

Figure 3.8 Multiple lenses combined to create a comprehensive view of why we should teach integrated STEM in context. *Source*: author created.

a comprehensive view of the benefits of learning and teaching integrated STEM in context.

Further, we have developed a case for using integrated STEM to address the practices of both the NGSS and CCSS-M. The efficiency of being able to address multiple practices, multiple concepts, a range of content, and increase student learning make teaching integrated STEM in context efficient and effective.

In addition, using a project-based contextual approach to address STEM curriculum and instruction is fun to teach! The excitement of the students, creativity of the assignment, and facilitator role of the teachers combine to provide a means to address twenty-first-century practices and progressive educational expectations in ways that lead to high levels of success. We encourage educators to consider innovative ways of addressing integrated STEM education, share their success and struggles, and continue to develop comprehensive STEM teaching and learning processes that address present and future needs of our students.

REFERENCES

Bransford, J. D., Brown, A. L., & Cocking, R. (2000). *How people learn: Brain, mind, experience, and school*. Washington, DC: National Academy Press.

Buck, L. B., Bretz, S. L., & Towns, M. H. (2008) Characterizing the level of inquiry in the undergraduate laboratory. *Journal of College Science Teaching, 38*(1), 52–58.

Carnevale, A. P., Smith, N., & Melton, M. (2011). STEM: Science, technology, engineering, mathematics. Washington, DC: Georgetown University Center on Education and the Workforce. Retrieved November 27, 2018, from https://cew.georgetown.edu/wp-content/uploads/2014/11/stem-complete.pdf.

Common Core State Standards Initiative. (2010). Common Core State standards for mathematics. Retrieved November 27, 2018, from http://www.corestandards.org/wp-content/uploads/Math_Standards1.pdf.

Haskell, R. E. (2001). *Transfer of learning: Cognition, instruction, and reasoning*. San Diego, CA: Academic Press.

Hoffmann-Riem, H., Biber-Klemm, S., Grossenbacher-Mansuy, W., Joye, D., Pohl, C., Wiesmann, U., & Zemp, E. (Eds.). (2008). *Handbook of transdisciplinary research*. Dordrecht, Netherlands: Springer.

Mayes, R., & Koballa Jr., T. R. (2012). Exploring the science framework. *Science & Children, 50*(4), 8–15.

Nadelson, L. S., Seifert, A., Moll, A., & Coats, B. (2012). i-STEM summer institute: An integrated approach to teacher professional development in STEM. *Journal of STEM Education: Innovation and Outreach, 13*(2), 69–83.

Nadelson, L. S., Seifert, A. L., & Hettinger, J. K. (2012). *If they come, they will build it! Focusing on engineering design as part of K–12 teacher STEM professional development.* Proceedings of the American Society of Engineering Education, San Antonio, TX, June 10–13.

Nadelson, L. S., Seifert, A. L., & Chang, C. (2013). The perceptions, engagement, and practices of teachers seeking professional development in place-based integrated STEM. *Teacher Education and Practice, 26*(2), 242–265.

Nadelson, L. S., & Seifert, A. L. (2014). Place based STEM: Leveraging local resources to engage K–12 teachers in teaching integrated STEM and for addressing the local STEM pipeline. Presented at the ASEE Annual Conference and Exposition by American Society of Engineering Education, Indianapolis, IN, June 15–18.

NGSS Lead States. (2013). *Next generation science standards: For states, by states.* Washington, DC: The National Academies Press.

Chapter 4

"I Don't Know Anything about DNA. Well I Do, but Not from You Guys"

A Vision for Interdisciplinary STEM Teaching

Vanessa Svihla, Kersti Tyson, Justin Boyle,
Jamie Collins, Ara Winter, Ayesha Livingston,
Abigail Stiles, and Julie Bryant

An increasing focus on science, technology, engineering, and math (STEM) practices (table 4.1) is evident in the Common Core State Standards for Mathematics (CCSS-M; Common Core State Standards Initiative, 2010) and the Next Generation Science Standards (NGSS Lead States, 2013). Although many state standards have previously included *practices*, tests have overwhelmingly emphasized facts and concepts.

Most states have likewise had a vast number of content standards to be covered (Schmidt, McKnight, & Raizen, 1997), leaving little room to deeply engage students in STEM practices. We choose to see the new standards as an opportunity to cover less content in greater depth, with a focus on understanding, and also as an opportunity to meaningfully and authentically engage students in STEM practices.

In the past, efforts to engage students in STEM practices have focused on *canonical* approaches. For instance, in science classrooms, this is the familiar Scientific Method. Although this has provided students with opportunities to *solve* problems posed by others, students have rarely had opportunities to ask their own questions and plan their own investigations; the "correct" answer is often known before students even begin.

Likewise, in US math classrooms, there has been an emphasis on solving problems using standard algorithms as a procedural process, and students

Table 4.1 STEM Practices from the Common Core State Standards for Mathematics and the Next Generation Science Standards

Math Practices	Science and Engineering Practices
1. Make sense of problems and persevere in solving them	1. Asking questions (for science) and defining problems (for engineering)
2. Reason abstractly and quantitatively	2. Developing and using models
3. Construct viable arguments and critique the reasoning of others	3. Planning and carrying out investigations
4. Model with mathematics	4. Analyzing and interpreting data
5. Use appropriate tools strategically	5. Using mathematics and computational thinking
6. Attend to precision	6. Constructing explanations (for science) and designing solutions (for engineering)
7. Look for and make use of structure	7. Engaging in argument from evidence
8. Look for and express regularity in repeated reasoning	8. Obtaining, evaluating, and communicating information

have rarely had opportunities to construct conceptual understanding of algorithms or develop their own ways to solve problems.

Research on how people learn and reform efforts both point toward a different approach to teaching and learning mathematics (Boerst, Sleep, Ball, & Bass, 2011; National Council of Teachers of Mathematics, 2000) and science (e.g., National Research Council [NRC], 2012): an approach that is grounded in inquiry (e.g., Furtak, Seidel, Iverson, & Briggs, 2012) and problem solving (e.g., Lampert, 2001; Schoenfeld, 2013). These efforts contributed to the articulation of practice standards in both the CCSS-M and the NGSS. The call for change is evident; the challenge facing educators is to learn what these changes look like in practice for both teachers and students.

In this chapter, we argue that engaging students in *all* the practices articulated in the CCSS-M and NGSS is an important way to help them to develop understanding, but we also know how different and difficult this work can be for teachers to accomplish. Most teachers have had few opportunities to experience these practices themselves, much less to support students to engage in these rich, but complex practices. Teachers may *intend* to engage their students in STEM practices, yet they may abandon a planned activity in response to concerns about covering the curriculum (Lakkala, Lallimo, & Hakkarainen, 2005) and compliance (Valli & Buese, 2007).

At the heart of our argument lies a reconceptualization of learning. Learning is not directly derived from teaching; instead, learning is understood as increasing participation in communities of practice (Lave & Wenger, 1991). This view of learning decenters the teacher and sharpens the focus on practices; instead of the "sage on the stage," the teacher becomes a more experienced member of the community of practice who can guide and support students' learning in that community. Students and teachers "share understandings concerning what they are doing and what that means in their lives and for their communities" (Lave & Wenger, 1991, p. 98).

Thus, studying productive communities of practice—whether they are professional research laboratories or fourth-grade math classrooms—can uncover ways that teaching supports learning (Lave, 1996). This stance implies that students in the community also learn from one another; we see interdisciplinary settings as particularly likely to foster such learning. As quoted in the chapter's title, Elena, a student in an interdisciplinary research lab states, "I don't know anything about DNA. Well I do, but not from you guys."

INTERDISCIPLINARY STEM PRACTICES

The NGSS and CCSS-M practice standards complement one another and support students' opportunities in STEM. An interdisciplinary approach to STEM has the potential to be more relevant because the "problems of society ... seldom come in discipline-shaped chunks" (Petrie, 1992, p. 327).

Furthermore, research suggests that interdisciplinary STEM learning experiences may be particularly beneficial to struggling students and to students who might not otherwise see themselves as scientists, mathematicians, and engineers (e.g., MacMath, Roberts, Wallace, & Chi, 2010). Not only does interdisciplinary STEM increase access to science and mathematics, but it also offers students more opportunities for revisiting and applying what they are learning.

In this chapter, we focus on practices in interdisciplinary contexts to illuminate the work teachers and students accomplish in these communities of practice. We present three exemplars that highlight pedagogical moves that support or inhibit students' participation in STEM practices. We begin in a professional laboratory setting at a university to describe and better understand these practices.

Next, we turn to a fourth-grade classroom during a mathematics lesson where students are engaging in these practices. Then, we present another professional laboratory setting to highlight particular challenges. We compare these settings to consider the potential for rich, complex practices in K–12 settings. We invite the reader to consider the same questions we asked ourselves:

- Do the practices occur in canonical, sequential fashion, like the well-known Scientific Method or standard mathematical algorithms?
- Can we observe both math and science practices at the same time?
- Do the practices that are bundled, such as "planning and carrying out investigations," happen as a bundled set?

- Do teachers control certain practices? Do students engage in the same practices as teachers?
- Do the students understand why they are engaged in the practices?

We also ask what of the professional laboratory should and can be practiced in classrooms? As noted elsewhere, there are important differences between professional labs and classrooms (O'Connor, Godfrey, & Moses, 1998).

However, we encourage the reader to have vision, to set aside expectations based on previous experience about what is possible in schools, and instead, take this as an opportunity to explore other possibilities. For each exemplar, we begin with guiding questions to orient the reader. Our aim is to show how understandings, decisions, and progress are guided and negotiated, providing clearer models of productive STEM practices *in practice*.

Exemplar 1:
INTERDISCIPLINARY SCIENCE LAB

Can you see the familiar Scientific Method?
Can you find both science and math practices?

Denise leads an interdisciplinary university research lab with a diverse group of eight undergraduate and graduate students. They all study caves, but they are bringing various perspectives together as they do their work. The lab conducts paradigm-shifting work on the role bacteria have played in forming caves. Here, they discuss microscopic objects they have found growing in caves; because of their shape, they are referred to as *stars*.

Denise: You could take TEM [transmission electron microscopy], slice 'em in half and see if there was a cell core.... But we've never been able to slice through the stars.

Mark: So that's what I was wondering. How these, like, stars are produced?

Denise: I don't know, but [another scientist] was able to get 'em produced in cultures [meaning he grew similar shapes in a petri dish-like environment].

Mark: So you're saying that cells are encased in?

Denise: They could be. To prove that you would have to be able to slice through them.

First, we describe the STEM practices we see here (noted in italics). Denise begins by jointly referencing *planning investigations* ("You could take") and the *appropriate tool use* (TEM). She next begins to *define the problem* ("But we've never been able to"). Mark then jointly *makes sense of the problem* and *asks a question*.

Denise then begins to *argue from evidence* ("able to get 'em produced in cultures"), which causes Mark to continue to *make sense of the problem* ("So you're saying") and *interpret data* ("that cells are encased in?"). Although he is also asking a question, it is not a science question like his previous question, but rather it is a request for information so that he can better understand the problem.

Denise's last comments bring the conversation back to a similar place it began: jointly *planning an investigation* ("To prove that you would") and *using tools appropriately* ("to slice through"). This exchange is representative of the lab meetings, with overlap of science and math practices a ubiquitous phenomenon. Although this lab is clearly engaged in science, it is difficult to see the familiar Scientific Method. Instead of occurring in a tidy sequence, we see the STEM practices unfolding in a rather nonlinear process.

In the next vignette, we again see overlapping science and math practices, but we also see something interesting happen as Tania brings a new idea to the lab and Denise considers it. Tania is working on a project studying deposits in caves that contain a lot of iron and manganese to learn how bacteria might be involved.

Tania: Is there? Does like, iron or manganese, or is there an assay [a type of test] out there that can measure, like, the light coming off of it? So I had this idea. I went to this "stars and constellation" talk. Totally different. Not my field. But someone—one of the speakers spoke about how they look at the color of light that is being emitted that would help tell the mass of the star.

Denise: Okay.

Tania: And I am wondering if there is something similar where—

Denise: Hmm!

Tania: bacteria, if they are emitting a light or a, compound, that maybe you could? I don't know.

Denise: There may be something along—

Tania: Maybe something out there that could at least tell us what it looks like?

Denise: That's interesting. This may be some of the techniques I just don't know, but it would be worth. . . . One of the ways to make progress on something like this is to look at what other fields do.

In this vignette, we see Tania begin by *asking questions*, *defining the problem*, and *communicating information* about the relationship between the color of light and mass. As Denise responds, encouraging but non-specific ("okay" and "Hmm!"), it falls to Tania to *make sense of* and *communicate* the problem she is *defining*.

In her last comment, Denise begins by indicating that she does not know enough to *evaluate* the usefulness of this idea ("I just don't know"), but then encourages Tania to *obtain and evaluate information* ("look at what other fields do"). After this exchange, Denise goes on to provide suggestions about isotopes that might be detectable with such a technique, which gives Tania an idea:

Tania: I have read a paper where they were looking at siderophores [compounds secreted by the bacteria they study] and when it binds it gives off its own wavelength.

Denise: Okay.

Tania: So, and I think they had used, like, the photo-

Denise: That could be a way to detect your siderophores.

Tania: Photo-? Spectrophotom-? Whatever that is?

Denise: Spectrophotometers?

Tania: Spectrophotometer was. But I know they were able to see the shift in light when it was bound.

Denise: Now, this would be worth pursuing. Especially for you. You might have an in-cave detector.

As the conversation unfolds, we see Tania and Denise *constructing viable arguments/explanations* about whether Tania's idea has merit ("when it binds"), *communicating information* about siderophores, beginning to *plan an investigation*, considering ways to *use tools strategically* ("Spectrophotometers"), and *designing a solution* ("an in-cave detector").

Again, we do not see the canonical Scientific Method occurring. We do see overlapping science and math practices. We also note that Tania has the opportunity to define her own problem. Across our observations, we see the teacher and students participate equally in the STEM practices and times when the practice is almost entirely in the student control, with guidance and encouragement from the teacher. This tells us that the students have opportunities to engage in the practices, and they understand why they are doing what they are doing. But how could this happen in a K–12 classroom?

Exemplar 2:
FOURTH-GRADE MATH

Can you find mathematical and science practices?
How is Ms. Martinez's classroom different from Denise's lab?

Next, we turn to a fourth-grade classroom in a highly diverse, high-poverty urban school in the northwestern United States. The teacher, Ms. Martinez, is in her fifth year of teaching. The vignette we present is from the last quarter of the school year. Students in this class were encouraged to solve math problems using multiple and alternative strategies. In this case, the class had been asked to solve three double-digit math problems using a specific strategy called the "box method."

The box method provides students with a strategy to decompose the numbers in the problem into tens and ones. Once all the students had solved the problems individually, the class gathered at the front of the room, and three students wrote their work on the board. It is important to note that it was an established norm in the class that the student whose work was being considered did not explain his or her work. Instead, the student stood by while his or her classmates considered the work and whether it made sense.

The following vignette marks the beginning of the discussion about the third solution, which was Gabriel's. He chose to multiply 50 × 45 by multiplying 50 × 40 and 50 × 5. Maggie wonders about this decision:

Maggie: How come you did 50 and 0, when you are doing the box method, aren't you supposed to break all the numbers apart?

Ms. Martinez: I'm so glad you asked that. I'm so glad that question came out.

Gabriel: Maggie, because over here—I got 50 and I just did it this way because I didn't know what way to do it, so I just . . .

Maggie: You could do 30 and 20.

Gabriel: That is not the number—

Jerome: Yeah it is.

Gabriel: that you multiply by.

Jerome: Yeah it is. It's the same number.

Maggie: 30 + 20 = 50. 3 + 2 = 5. Just add the two zeros to 3 and 2 and it will be 30 and 20, 30, 40, 50 (counting it out on her hand).

Ms. Martinez: So Maggie, are you suggesting that he decompose 50 into 30 and 20? Is that what you did? On your paper? Is that the only way to do it?

Maggie: There is also 10 and 40.

Ms. Martinez: Any other way? So are you still saying that 50 and 0 is wrong?

Maggie: Mmhmm.

Ms. Martinez: Let's talk about that.

In this vignette, we see multiple STEM practices enacted. Maggie begins by *asking a question* ("How come you did 50 and 0"), and Ms. Martinez encourages her and the class by saying, "I'm so glad you asked that."

Maggie, Jerome, Gabriel, and Ms. Martinez each *make sense of the problem.* To do so, they *obtain and evaluate information* and *reason abstractly and quantitatively* about Gabriel's solution, "50 and 0." In their reasoning, they *engage in argument from evidence* (e.g., Maggie's "30 + 20 = 50"). Both Gabriel and Maggie *construct explanations* about their work. Jerome and Maggie *critique the reasoning of others*, whereas Jerome *attends to precision* ("Yeah, it is. It's the same number").

Ms. Martinez encourages each student to respond to Maggie's assertion when she says, "Let's talk about that." She detours from her lesson plan to explore Maggie's question in depth, guiding and supporting students to seek to understand one another's thinking. As the discussion continues, we see this happen.

For example, Diana defends Gabriel's proposal: "You have to break them up into the 10s and the 1s, and there is no 1 in the 1s place, so he just puts a zero." In this statement, we see her *analyzing the data* presented by her classmates and *critiquing their reasoning*, while arguing for the *appropriate and strategic use of the tool* (the box method) that they were asked to use. Not only is Diana making sense of the math at hand, she is making sense of Gabriel's thinking about the math in light of how she understands the box method.

Another student, Oswaldo, asserts similar reasoning: "Because you can't put 30 and 20 and come up with the same answers, because that is saying that 30 is in the tens column and 20 is in the ones column. You can't do that because it has to be in the right column. So what you could . . . do is 50 in the 10s, the zero is in the ones column so then that is right. But 30 and 20 isn't because 30 is in the ten—the right column, but 20 is not."

Oswaldo, like Diana, is *analyzing the data* presented by his classmates and *critiquing their reasoning*; he is also more clearly *constructing an explanation* as part of his *critique* ("because it has to be in the right column"), and *making use of structure* of place value to *design a solution* ("So what you could . . . do"). Both Diana and Oswaldo are *looking for and seeking to express regularity in repeated reasoning* as they first *critique* then *design solutions* to the problem at hand—building a response to Maggie's assertion that using "50 and 0 is wrong."

After several students had *constructed explanations* as they sought to *make sense of the problem*, Gabriel jumps back into the discussion excitedly, "I know why she put, I know why you put 20 because (he gets up and goes to board) this is saying that there is 20 ones in that and right here 30 tens, no 3 tens and right here is 20 ones." In his comments, we see that he *interprets the data* that various students had *communicated* and is able to *make sense of how* Maggie *solved her problem* ("I know why she put"); Gabriel *models his thinking mathematically* (as he draws on the board) and is able to *use mathematics* to *construct an argument* about someone else's thinking, Maggie's.

Once Gabriel *constructs a viable argument* about Maggie's solution, other students can *make sense* of both Gabriel's and Maggie's solutions. The class continues to discuss and *construct an explanation* as they work to make sense of how both students could be right, even though they used different numbers to get the same answer. To support this direction, Ms. Martinez asks her students to go one step further, to *interpret the data* presented thus far in the discussion and *to look for and express regularity in repeated reasoning*; she asks her class to consider, "Is there a rule that you could come up with?"

This discussion leaks into "writing time," but the students have still not quite *constructed a* full *explanation* for a rule to describe their observations. To wrap up the discussion, Ms. Martinez decides to summarize the mathematics discussion that took place:

Ms. Martinez: But they [one of the groups] were talking about breaking the numbers up and it doesn't really matter how you break them up. And then Maggie and Gabriel were having the same conversation. So they tested their thinking, which is so smart to try it with another problem, [addressing the researcher] isn't that so smart? So they test it with another problem and they made it up and they did 54 times 70 and Maggie tried it her way, Gabriel tried it his way, again they got the same thing, but then they said this, "You can probably break up the numbers any way that you want to as long as you have [the right numbers]" and then Gabriel said, "I wonder if you have 72 times 54." So we were looking at 72 times 54. Everyone say 72 × 54."

Class: 72 × 54

Ms. Martinez: So they, Gabriel said, "Hey, I wonder if you can do 71 and 1 times 50 and 4?"

Gabriel: And you can break 50 into 25 and 25.

Ms. Martinez: And then he said you can probably even break up the 50 into 25 and 25 and 4.

Class: (oohs and aahs)

Alexia: They made up their own—that's not even a box that's a rectangle

Ms. Martinez: So it is like we are extending the box strategy, and Seraphina had the same thinking with this 100s, how she took it, but Kalista said well it wouldn't be the box strategy anymore that would be the rectangle strategy. Which is so true.

Across these discussions, we see the students in this fourth-grade class, with the support of their teacher, work to *make sense of problems* by *constructing an explanation* about how two students got the same answer but decomposed the original problem into different numbers. We also see overlapping math and science practices.

In both the interdisciplinary research lab and the fourth-grade classroom, the teacher proposes questions related to their observations and encourages further exploration. Both Denise and Ms. Martinez ask questions that direct students toward inquiry and problem solving. These exemplars highlight how *problematizing* the subject matter can engage both the teacher and students in intellectual curiosity and discovery through discussion.

Similar to Denise's lab, we see times when the practice is almost entirely in the students' control with guidance and encouragement from the teacher. This tells us that the students have opportunities to engage in the practices, and they understand *why* they are doing what they are doing. Compared to Denise's lab, Ms. Martinez's classroom offers students more opportunities to talk directly to one another, something Ms. Martinez nurtures and encourages. Both exemplars begin from a student's question as the focus of inquiry, unplanned but guided by the teacher.

We also see that Ms. Martinez and the students—like in Denise's lab—participate in the *same* STEM practices, meaning *everyone* in the class has opportunities to ask questions, define problems, and make sense of problems. What happens when this is not the case? To understand more about what works, it sometimes helps to consider what does not work. We, therefore, provide an exemplar to help illustrate the importance of *participation* in the interdisciplinary STEM practices to support learning. Our third exemplar provides this contrast to the first two exemplars.

Exemplar 3:
COMPUTER SCIENCE RESEARCH LAB

What happens when students and teachers have different opportunities to participate in STEM practices?

Jack leads a research group of five university graduate students who are learning advanced mathematics (i.e., linear algebra, matrices) to solve complex computer science problems. He teaches through projects because he wants his students to solve real problems themselves.

We share a brief vignette of exchanges between Jack and Shaun. Although there are four other students in the lab, they almost never speak up during meetings. In this vignette, Jack uses complex, advanced mathematical terms related to matrices; we encourage the reader to *see through* these terms and to focus on who engages in particular practices. Do Jack and Shaun engage in the same practices? How is the participation in this vignette similar or different to the first two exemplars?

Jack: So basically, I'm looking for something now that goes—that goes [speaking and writing out mathematical notation] v-b, um, x dot v-b plus v-a x dot v-a, okay. But it's not an operator is it? It's just a formula. It's not really an operator yet.

Shaun: Yeah.

Jack: It's certainly not the matrix operator that I want. So now the game is to, to set it up so I have *this* case. I am looking for an m [a matrix], put that [writing m=mx on the board]: mx is equal to that. I'm looking for an equivalency. Can you find an m, a matrix m, that takes us directly to that projection?

Shaun: So, so?

Jack: That's the game. That is really what I was asking for. If you started with this simple m [matrix], this simple of a representation you should be able to do it, right?

Shaun: So this is a, this is a, so, umm, so, this is where, last time, you were asking us about the, umm, for example, our reflection direction, umm?

In this vignette we first see that Jack is *communicating* his *reasoning* to Shaun and the other students in the room. In doing so, he is *defining the problem* to be solved ("I'm looking for something now that goes"). He is also *reasoning abstractly and quantitatively* as he defines and communicates.

As Shaun engages with these ideas, he is *making sense of the problem* that Jack has *framed* for him. Shaun follows Jack's initial comments, agreeing with him that, "It's not really an operator yet." As Jack continues to *define the problem* ("So now the game is to"), he attends to *structure,* and then he *asks a question* ("Can you find an m, a matrix m"). Shaun's response ("So, so?") tells us that he is still trying to *make sense of the problem.*

Jack continues to define the problem ("That is really what I was asking"), but he also suggests *using a model* ("If you started with this simple") to solve the problem. Shaun's stammering response shows us that he is still *making sense of the problem* by *obtaining information.*

In contrast to Mark's question in the interdisciplinary science lab ("How these, like, stars are produced?") or Maggie's question in the fourth-grade class ("How come you did 50 and 0?"), which helped us see that posing questions was a safe practice for students; here, we see Shaun's contributions as rather meager, and his last contribution as uncertain and not generative. This response reflects the expectation given by Jack that what he has offered is "simple," and therefore that Shaun ought to be able to follow Jack's reasoning.

Across this conversation, we see that Jack has *made sense of the problem* and has *made use of structure,* but Shaun does not understand the problem and works to follow Jack's *reasoning* about this problem he does not understand. In other words, Jack has already *defined, investigated,* and *identified mathematical structure* with respect to this problem.

He is *communicating* his *reasoning* without providing time or support for Shaun or the other students in the room to *define, investigate,* or *seek mathematical structure* in a problem of their own. Because Jack thinks the problem is simple, he assumes it is simple for his students. Rather than being curious about his students' thinking, as Denise and Ms. Martinez are, Jack seeks for his students to understand his thinking alone.

Here again, we see the practices occurring in a messy, nonlinear manner, rather than reflecting the canonical representation of science or math practice. Likewise, the practices overlap with one another. But this vignette also highlights another important dimension: as written in the NGSS and CCSS-M, some of the practices are *bundled*; for instance, "Planning and carrying out investigations," or "Developing and using models." Although we see lots of practices overlapping, we rarely see the bundled practices happening at the same time.

Planning is a different practice than *carrying out an investigation*. We see from Jack and Shaun's interactions that Jack is the one who gets to *plan and define*, and Shaun works to understand the problem so that he can *carry out the investigation* presented to him, even though Jack already knows the solution.

This is a common situation in school settings; the problem and solution are known at the outset, and it is up to the student to follow the teacher or textbook solution method. We question this model because we do not see evidence that Shaun develops the type of understanding demanded by NGSS and CCSS-M in the same way that we see it in the first two exemplars.

Although the projects are meaningful and relevant from Jack's point of view, this is not always the case for his students. Because he has not revealed *why* his approaches are useful and the students have not been involved in defining the problem, their involvement in STEM practices is constrained and though they diligently make progress on this work, the activities are rendered inauthentic.

Ultimately, in Jack's research group, students occupy limited spaces; they have permission to act and think, but it is Jack who gets to define and solve the problems. Shaun may work to follow Jack's reasoning, but because it is not his own, the ideas he takes up are taken up only temporarily and too-easily discarded. In one case, Jack explains his thinking about a problem for seven minutes, after which Shaun asks: "What's the goal of it what are we trying to do?" Without understanding that goal, it is unlikely Shaun will retain whatever understanding he might have absorbed.

SHIFTING PRACTICES, PROVIDING TIME, ENGAGING, AND THINKING TOGETHER

The three exemplars shared in this chapter highlight how teachers (Jack, Denise, & Ms. Martinez) are working to move beyond traditional instructional methods to enact STEM practices. Although Jack is the least successful, he did start in a productive direction with an authentic problem and tried to engage his students in deep understanding.

To really support deep understanding, Jack needs to *shift* his own teaching practice to allow his students more access to the STEM practices. In particular, his students need opportunities to define the problem and time to engage in making progress on solving the problem *on their own*, so that they can engage in thinking *together* and as a means to gain understanding.

It is evident that Ms. Martinez provided her students time to work on the problem on their own before the conversation. This allowed the students to think together and critique each other's reasoning. Instead of prioritizing learning a single, canonical solution (e.g., the right answer using the right process), Ms. Martinez wanted her students to learn that there are multiple ways to decompose fifty beyond grouping into tens and ones.

To support this, she made deliberate decisions about which student work was shared; by choosing different solution methods and supporting students to understand one another's thinking, she created a safe space and provided time for students to engage in the STEM practices together.

As a result, these fourth-grade students were not just agreeing (like in Jack's lab), but they were able to apply their new understanding; they generated and decomposed numbers to test their newfound understanding that "you can probably break up the numbers any way that you want." By engaging *together* in the practices, they worked to understand one another's thinking, and in doing so, deepened their conceptual understanding of numbers, even when students were initially thought to be wrong.

Likewise, in Denise's lab, the students engaged *with* Denise to plan investigations. Both Denise's and Ms. Martinez's approaches allowed the students to learn what it means to do science and math authentically, as a messy process that includes missteps, guesses, and retries to answer questions. Both provided time for students to bring in their own ideas and encouraged those ideas even when they could not evaluate their value.

We see a lesson for teachers in Denise's and Ms. Martinez's encouragement of these nascent ideas; when faced with a wrong idea, a misconception or naive conception, instead of dismissing it, consider treating it as Denise treated Tania's idea or Ms. Martinez treated Maggie's idea. Encourage the students to critically evaluate their own ideas, rather than, as Jack often asked of his students, "I will show that, but maybe you can believe me?"

MORAL TO THE STORY:
Creating Opportunities to Practice Practices

We have shared three exemplars of teaching and learning through interdisciplinary STEM practices. It may be easy to dismiss the idea of enacting the instruction visible in Denise's lab as not feasible in K–12 classrooms because Denise's students are capable, interested university students. However, based on the other exemplars we shared, this is neither necessary nor sufficient for allowing students to engage in and learn from STEM practices.

In fact, Jack's students come from a far more selected or selective group, and Ms. Martinez's students come from a far less selected or selective group. We take a stance that *every* student deserves the opportunity to engage in STEM practices to learn content authentically. However, we acknowledge how difficult this instructional shift is to enact, especially for teachers who have not been provided opportunities to learn to teach from this pedagogical perspective. Thus, we next consider the consequences for more conventional approaches.

When the teacher is the authority and the students' role is to consume information, learning is "tidy," meaning the students are presented with specific methods to "practice." However, when a *practice* becomes something to simply and *rotely* (without meaning) practice, this results in a misunderstanding of STEM practices, and this has consequences. Consider, for example, Elena, a student in Denise's lab. Elena was the first person in her family to attend college. In high school she became well-versed and successful in the Scientific Method, and based on that success, she decided to pursue a science career.

Students like Elena are less likely to have had access to out-of-school and home experiences that disrupt this tidy view of science. When faced with the nonlinear, nondeterministic, messiness of actual STEM practices, Elena might easily decide, "I must be doing this wrong. I must be bad at science" and make the choice to abandon what had been a promising career path. We see this as a loss—both to students like Elena, and to STEM fields, which could benefit from increased diversity.

Consider as well, Shaun's response to one of Jack's explanations: "I just never would have, I just don't, I just wouldn't have gotten there on my own, from right here, to right there. I wouldn't have gone there because I don't. . . ." Without opportunities to *try* to get there, how will he ever get there? A similar breakdown happens when students become adept at using a standard algorithm for addition, subtraction, multiplication, and division. Many students can solve the problems, but they lack a conceptual understanding of what is occurring mathematically. Thus, when they get to algebra and more advanced mathematics that depend on the conceptual understanding, these students falter.

This is important because it has an impact on who believes that they can "do" science or math, and in the long term, it impacts who believes they belong in STEM fields. In science and math, messiness and being wrong is an important part of the process. It is rare for a hypothesis to be supported on a first try, but failures to support it provide important information about what works and what does not. STEM learning environments that incorporate practices authentically are "messy"; they allow students to engage with context, make mistakes, and make sense of concepts (O'Connor et al., 1998).

INTERDISCIPLINARY PRACTICES PROVIDE POINTS OF ENTRY

Interdisciplinary STEM can provide points of entry for students. First, this is because interdisciplinary problems provide opportunities for students to be exposed to new practices or to engage practices and ideas learned elsewhere. Second, interdisciplinary STEM requires that teachers and students alike engage, and be encouraged to engage, in each other's thinking.

In Denise's lab, Denise shows that she is curious about her students' thinking and ideas. In the fourth-grade classroom, Ms. Martinez has worked to build a community of practice where students are encouraged to be curious about one another's sense making. But in Jack's lab, the emphasis is on students understanding Jack's thinking. By changing whose ideas are worth attending to, we see a shift in who engages in practices and who has opportunities to develop understanding. It changes the teacher's focus to facilitating inquiry and seeking to understand students' emergent and sometimes stumbling thinking. If their learning through STEM practices is sustained into college, Ms. Martinez's students would likely be successful in Denise's lab, but less so in Jack's.

PEDAGOGICAL APPROACHES

These three exemplars can provide teachers with an opportunity to think about how engaging in STEM practices can support understanding. We make salient a few characteristics and differences across the exemplars to help teachers envision ways to bring practices into their classrooms in authentic ways. This involves taking time, shifting practice, seeking worthwhile complex learning experiences, and allowing practices to showcase the messiness of STEM.

First, as we saw in the exemplars, allowing students to engage in and learn from the practices takes time; time many teachers may believe they do not have. We advocate for teachers to see the new standards as an opportunity to *take*, to borrow through an interdisciplinary approach or steal if need be, that time. Instead of reviewing facts and concepts not learned the previous years, take time to allow students to develop understanding.

Second, for students to develop this type of understanding, many teachers may find that shifting practice is needed. The students in Jack's lab were confused and mostly non-participatory, suggesting that they neither understood the mathematical concepts nor why they were doing what they were doing. Ms. Martinez's and Denise's students had the opportunity to define the problems they were solving. They engaged in all the practices with their teachers. True discovery learning means that both students and teacher are engaged with a novel problem.

Although this may be the case in Denise's lab, it was not true in Jack's lab; he had already found the solution he desired. While double-digit multiplication is not novel to Ms. Martinez, it is to her students, and she promotes discovery as she and her students discover each other's thinking. When the teacher has more knowledge of the solution at the outset, as Jack and Ms. Martinez both do, he or she can still support students by listening to understand how they are thinking, as opposed to promoting a particular solution path that does not connect to student ideas. Patience and curiosity are essential for allowing students to authentically engage in the STEM practices.

Third, we encourage teachers to seek opportunities for students in the form of complex, worthwhile, authentically intellectual problems that are co-constructed by students. Learning basic facts and concepts can happen along the way to defining and solving complex problems.

Fourth, by allowing students to engage in the *messiness* of STEM practices, students can develop a better understanding of actual STEM practice. This allows them to make more informed decisions about career choices. Therefore, we recommend that teachers design learning experiences that allow students to engage in the STEM practices. It is likely that your own and your colleagues' first attempts may be uncomfortable and messy, but remind yourself that learning, like STEM, is not a linear, tidy process, and persevere. Be as curious about your students' thinking as you want them to be about the learning at hand.

As a teacher, you may not know what is possible for you and your students until you have the opportunity to try. Further, like any new practice, you may falter and struggle, and your students may initially resist. This is difficult work. We encourage you to *choose* to have vision for yourself and your students, as President John F. Kennedy (1962) explained about choosing to go to the moon "because that goal will serve to organize and measure the best of our energies and skills, because that challenge is one that we are willing to accept, one we are unwilling to postpone, and one which we intend to win."

We urge you to consider two questions that guide our own ongoing work in the process of transforming our own pedagogical practices: "When do we give our students permission to be thinking and contributing beings?" and "What are our assumptions about what our students can do and think and know?"

CONCLUSIONS

Finally, we leave you to consider that in Jack's lab, the students did not know why they were doing what they were doing, and Jack had to work hard to keep them going; it is effortful, tiring work to pull students in a direction they cannot fathom. In contrast, Denise's lab and Ms. Martinez's classroom were fun, joyful, and safe spaces, where students could be themselves and explore new roles and identities. We wish the latter for your current and future students as well as our own.

REFERENCES

Boerst, T. A., Sleep, L., Ball, D. L., & Bass, H. (2011). Preparing teachers to lead mathematics discussions. *Teachers College Record, 113*(12), 2844–2877.

Common Core State Standards Initiative. (2010). Common Core State standards for mathematics. Retrieved November 27, 2018, from http://www.corestandards.org/wp-content/uploads/Math_Standards1.pdf.

Furtak, E. M., Seidel, T., Iverson, H., & Briggs, D. C. (2012). Experimental and quasi-experimental studies of inquiry-based science teaching a meta-analysis. *Review of Educational Research, 82*(3), 300–329.

Kennedy, J. F. (1962). Address at Rice University, Houston, Texas, September 12, 1962. Speech presented at Rice Stadium, Houston, Texas. Retrieved November 27, 2018, from https://www.jfklibrary.org/Asset-Viewer/Archives/JFKPOF-040-001.aspx.

Lakkala, M., Lallimo, J., & Hakkarainen, K. (2005). Teachers' pedagogical designs for technology-supported collective inquiry: A national case study. *Computers & Education, 45*(3), 337–356.

Lampert, M. (2001). *Teaching problems and the problems of teaching*. New Haven, CT: Yale University Press.

Lave, J. (1996). Teaching, as learning, in practice. *Mind, Culture, and Activity, 3*(3), 149–164.

Lave, J., & Wenger, E. (1991). *Situated learning: Legitimate peripheral participation*. Cambridge, UK: Cambridge University Press.

MacMath, S., Roberts, J., Wallace, J., & Chi, X. (2010). Research section: Curriculum integration and at-risk students: a Canadian case study examining student learning and motivation. *British Journal of Special Education, 37*(2), 87–94.

National Council of Teachers of Mathematics. (2000). *Principles and standards for school mathematics* (vol. 1). Reston, VA: Author.

National Research Council (NRC). (2012). *A framework for K–12 science education: Practices, crosscutting concepts, and core ideas*. Washington, DC: The National Academies Press. https://doi.org/10.17226/13165.

NGSS Lead States. (2013). *Next generation science standards: For states, by states*. Washington, DC: The National Academies Press.

O'Connor, M. C., Godfrey, L., & Moses, R. P. (1998). The missing data point: Negotiating purposes in classroom mathematics and science. In J. Greeno and S. Goldman (Eds.), *Thinking practices in mathematics and science learning* (pp. 89–125). Hillsdale, NJ: Lawrence Erlbaum.

Petrie, H. G. (1992). Interdisciplinary Education: are we faced with insurmountable opportunities? *Review of Research in Education, 18*, 299–333.

Schmidt, W. H., McKnight, C. C., & Raizen, S. A. (1997). *A splintered vision: An investigation of US science and mathematics education*. Dordrecht, Netherlands: Kluwer Academic Publishers.

Schoenfeld, A. H. (2013). Reflections on problem solving theory and practice. *The Mathematics Enthusiast, 10*(1&2), 9–34.

Valli, L., & Buese, D. (2007). The changing roles of teachers in an era of high-stakes accountability. *American Educational Research Journal, 44*(3), 519–558.

Chapter 5

Mathematics, Science, and Technology Reform in Teacher Education

Implications for Teaching Practice

Deborah Moore-Russo and Noemi Waight

Future and current teachers enter education courses and professional-development opportunities with beliefs and opinions regarding schools and instruction (Millsaps, 2000; Phelps & Lee, 2003; Skott, 2001). The ideas they hold tend to be based on their experiences in their years of observation as students (Eiriksson, 1997; Lortie, 1975). Just as an individual's beliefs and priorities shape teaching (Skott, 2009), there are norms related to instruction that impact the entire teaching community. Ideas of appropriate classroom enactment are often based on teachers' acquisition of content in abstraction (Gallagher, 2007).

In this chapter, we propose that teacher education needs to promote an expanded view of teaching (Grossman & McDonald, 2008) that focuses on *teaching as a practice* rather than the *teacher as an individual*. This view focuses on the work of teaching (Selling, Garcia, & Ball, 2016) rather than the teacher as an individual.

By considering teaching as a practice with actions, customs, processes, and pursuits that are particular to the profession, in the same way that law and medicine are considered practices, teacher educators are positioned to help current and future teachers reconsider and alter the system of dispositions or the "feel for the game" (Bourdieu, 1998, p. 25) that influence their ideas on appropriate mathematics and science teaching.

PRACTICAL RATIONALITY

As the saying goes, a fish would be the last to notice water. The practical rationality that produces, regulates, and sustains any practice is so much a part of the engrained environment that practitioners are usually unaware of its existence (Herbst & Chazan, 2003). By practical rationality, we mean "the implicit relations, tacit conventions, subtle cues, untold rules of thumb, recognizable intuitions, specific perceptions, well-tuned sensitivities, embodied understandings, underlying assumptions, and shared world views" (Wenger, 1998, p. 47) held by those in the community of practice.

Even though the rationality that guides a practice is not explicitly taught, it is this practical rationality that "provides the regulatory framework that socializes its current and future practitioners into ways of thinking and acting that conform to expectations" (Moore-Russo & Weiss, 2011, p. 464).

The continuity of a practice comes from its structure and cohesion to a set of norms (i.e., archetypal behaviors that characterize the practice). Even though those within the community of practice typically hold common norms, it is rare that they are explicitly taught to novices. Lortie (1975) calls this an "apprenticeship of observation" where future teachers develop deep-seated ideas about the content and how it should be taught (including the role that technology should play).

Before they enter their first teacher education course, future teachers have experienced and are accustomed to the rationality that drives the practice of teaching. Therefore, their established ideas about teaching (Ball, 1988) tend to be resistant to change (Block & Hazelip, 1995; Kagan, 1992).

Future mathematics and science teachers have often encountered years of schooling in which students were expected to be passive listeners memorizing rules and transferring information from the teacher (Fosnot, 1989; Pajares, 1992; Phelps & Lee, 2003). Experiences such as these shape future teachers' beliefs and teaching (Millsaps, 2000; Renzaglia, Hutchins, & Lee, 1997; Skott, 2001). This sustains the norms that guide the practice of teaching by creating a cyclic continuity that is difficult to break.

When departures from norms do occur, they are typically identified and justified. The justification serves to reconfirm the norms while outlining the conditions when breaches are acceptable and further engrains the rationality that provides the persistent continuity of practice. Future teachers go on to teach as they were taught, often perpetuating the passive, information-transfer, rule-driven instructional environments they experienced. Any alternative instructional methods that breach normative behavior are employed sparingly and often seen as isolated incidents or special cases.

Reproductive Conceptions of Teaching

How teachers interpret their roles, the act of teaching, the nature of their disciplines, and the role of learners impact the decisions they make about their teaching practice (Hewson & Hewson, 1989). Koballa, Graber, Coleman, and Kemp (2000) reported that teacher conceptions—how teachers view and think about teaching and learning based on their prior experiences and practice—were for the most part reproductive rather than constructive. Essentially, *reproductive* conceptions are revealing of teacher-centered, didactic instructional approaches focused on content coverage where students are expected to reproduce teachers' ideas, methods, and so on.

Wiggins and McTighe (2005) caution that reproductive conceptions of teaching and learning are also embedded in misconceptions related to the process of instructional design. Teachers often reproduce the twin sins of instructional design: (1) focus on meaningless activities and (2) the notion that teachers have to "cover" content. In science, a traditional focus reproduces activities that are fun but generally fail to foster understanding.

A focus on coverage often emphasizes only information. In mathematics, we see students solving problems without understanding the conceptual connections between problems and solutions (Thompson, 2008). Unless explicit, practical experiences do not always challenge these conceptions; they endure and become perpetuated by the next generation of teachers.

MATHEMATICS IN THE CLASSROOM

Most in the mathematics education research community would agree with the following underlying assumptions. Mathematics is more than a static body of facts and rules to be transferred to individuals. It is dynamic way of thinking actively created by individuals (Cobb, Yackel, & Wood, 1992; von Glaserfeld, 1987). Learning is a social affair in which interactions provide individuals opportunities to make meaning of mathematical ideas (Cobb, Boufi, McClain, & Whitenack, 1997; Lave & Wenger, 1991) and to develop math habits of mind (Cuoco, Goldenberg, & Mark, 1996).

These assumptions undergird recent national recommendations for mathematics education in the United States (National Governors Association for Best Practices and Council of Chief State School Officers, 2010; National Council of Teachers of Mathematics, 1989, 2000, 2006). However, many teachers consider mathematics to be "a discipline with a priori rules and procedures that ... students have to learn by rote" (Handal, 2003, p. 54). For too many teachers, knowing mathematics is synonymous with symbol manipulation (Thompson, 1992) and being able to memorize and follow step-by-step procedures (Ball, 1988). This is because what is taken as

> mathematically normative in a classroom is constrained by the current goals, beliefs, suppositions, and assumptions of the classroom participants ... these

goals and largely implicit understandings are themselves influenced by what is legitimized as acceptable mathematical activity. (Yackel & Cobb, 1996, p. 460)

We are not promoting the false dichotomy between conceptual understanding and procedural skills (Kieran, 2013). However, holding mathematics as related to memorization and following steps discounts instructional practices that facilitate other strands of mathematical proficiency (National Research Council [NRC], 2001), such as adaptive reasoning, conceptual understanding, and strategic competence.

Mathematics teachers show evidence of a mind-set that differentiates between meaningful mathematical practices of mathematicians and of classroom mathematics (Liljedahl, 2008). Unfortunately, there is a misalignment between "acceptable mathematical activity" in many US classrooms and what has been called "authentic mathematical work" (Weiss, Herbst, & Chen, 2009). Silver (1994) noted that problem posing is a prominent feature of mathematical work. There should be a generative nature of mathematical engagement where inquiry and problem posing play roles just as important as problem solving (Weiss, 2009).

However, teachers do not expect their students "to develop mathematical meanings" or "to use meanings in their thinking" (Thompson, 2008, p. 45). Few mathematics classrooms include activities that allow for flexible mathematical thinking and inquiry. Students are presented with finalized definitions rather than opportunities to create, reflect on, and compare definitions (de Villiers, 1998). Students are neither asked to pose their own problems nor to generalize solutions for a specific problem to a broader class of problems (Moore-Russo, 2010). So, what might inspire mathematics teachers to adopt more inquiry-oriented practices?

Authentic Mathematical Work

Herbst and Chazan (2011) point out that understanding the practical rationality that guides mathematics instruction should help inform the mathematics education community as to what teachers regard as authentic mathematical work. If teachers consider authentic mathematical activity to be related to the work done by mathematicians, then they might recognize that their instructional goals should include the generation and refinement of existing mathematical ideas and methods (Weiss, 2009).

The mathematics community works together to push the field forward. If teachers recognize the true nature of mathematics and what constitutes authentic mathematical work, they are more likely to feel obligated to "steward a valid representation of the discipline of mathematics" (Herbst & Chazan, 2011, p. 450). Herbst and Balacheff (2009) drew attention to the *disciplinary obligation*—the obligation of a teacher to faithfully represent his or her discipline.

Cross (2009) found that there was a relationship between teachers' beliefs about mathematics and their beliefs about pedagogy and student learning. To help the next generation of teachers break current instructional cycles, teacher educators should provide experiences in which future teachers justify beliefs and actions that depart from the norms that drive mathematics instruction. Future teachers need activities that help them question instructional practices that limit mathematics to the individual acquisition of a static body of facts and rules.

Rather than considering mathematics instruction as facilitation of accumulated facts and procedural fluency, Thompson (2002) describes mathematics instruction as needing to create "a particular dynamical space . . . [that allows] for a variety of understandings" where the teacher choreographs conversations, which stimulate reflection and inquiry around the mathematical topics at hand (Thompson, 1985).

Cohen, Raudenbush, and Ball (2003) propose a conception of instruction that entails "interactions among teachers and students around content" (p. 122). If mathematics classrooms are to provide activities that portray mathematics as a generative, collaborative field then instructional design in mathematics should consider "the 'ways of thinking' that students bring to instruction and which might be leveraged profitably to move the conversation forward" (Silverman & Thompson, 2008, pp. 507–8).

Changing the Practice of Mathematics Education

Although engrained beliefs and the norms that drive a practice can be difficult to change, research has found that certain efforts produce changes in future and practicing teachers' conceptions of mathematics. Allowing practicing teachers to engage in definition construction has helped to bring changes in their ideas about the nature of mathematics and how it should be taught (Leikin & Winicki-Landman, 2001). Instead of supplying a finished definition, displaying different examples of a particular figure and tasking groups of teachers to create a definition represents authentic mathematical work.

Challenging future teachers' pedagogical conceptions (Feiman-Nemser & Buchmann, 1987) by providing examples of more authentic mathematical activity (e.g., Herbst & Chazan, 2011; Chazan, Sela, & Herbst, 2012) has been successful. Weiss and Moore-Russo (2012) outlines how this can be done by altering given conditions in a problem that show the generative nature of mathematical exploration.

One of the most successful methods for producing change is through future teachers' experiences with mathematical discovery, which has been shown to have a profound and immediate transformative effect on the beliefs regarding the nature of mathematics and the teaching and learning of mathematics (Liljedahl, 2005; Liljedahl, Rolka, & Rösken, 2007).

Mathematics teacher educators must realize that they "have the dual responsibility of preparing mathematics teachers, both *mathematically* and *pedagogically*" (Liljedahl, Chernoff, & Zazkis, 2007, p. 239). In fact, it has been suggested that "subject matter related goals and beliefs might be called *hard* and pedagogical content goals and beliefs *soft*" (Törner, Rolka, Rösken, & Sriraman, 2010, p. 416).

In other words, content issues seem to override pedagogical concerns (Wilson & Cooney, 2002). Therefore, it is imperative that teacher educators provide opportunities that make transparent the generative, inquiry-based nature of mathematics. To bridge the gap between what is legitimized as acceptable mathematical activity in classrooms and the work of mathematicians, teacher educators should capitalize on the disciplinary obligation by helping mathematics teachers come to better understand the true nature of mathematics.

SIMILAR TENSIONS AND PARTICULAR ISSUES IN SCIENCE EDUCATION AND TECHNOLOGY

Consistent with the challenges noted in mathematics education, enactment of authentic inquiry practices in K–12 science classrooms that focus on replicating scientific practices and habits of mind have lagged. The National Research Council (NRC; 2011) distinguishes between science as a body of knowledge and science as a "set of practices used to establish, extend, and refine that knowledge (pp. 2–3). This distinction serves as a reminder that science is not just about acquiring facts or coverage but rather it is a way of knowing. Science teaching and learning should reflect actual science practice.

With traditional orientations of instruction in teaching and technology integration persisting in classrooms (e.g., Gallagher, 2007; Waight & Abd-El-Khalick, 2011; Yerrick, Radosta, & Greene, 2018), there is a heightened urgency to help teachers understand that the natures of science and mathematics are not fixed, static entities (Popkewitz, 2000). Rather, both disciplines reflect dynamic construction of knowledge and promote authentic ways of knowing.

More than twenty years ago, Stinner (1992) cautioned that science instruction was following a reproductive conception of teaching where finished products of science were transmitted to students with an emphasis on *what* a person knew instead of *how* a person knew. To mitigate these effects Mathews (1998) suggested that science teachers "[should encourage] questions about what things can be known and how we can know them, and about what things actually exist in the world and the relations possible between them" (p. 169).

Even though the practical rationality lens has not been used in framing research in science education as it has in mathematics education, most would agree that tapping into the disciplinary obligation could be of benefit in science teacher education. Science education would benefit from teachers recognizing the nature of science as a discipline and what it means to engage in authentic scientific work.

Complex Nature of Scientific Inquiry

When students learn science, they "describe objects and events, ask questions, acquire knowledge, construct explanations of natural phenomena, test those explanations in many different ways, and communicate ideas to others" (NRC, 2011, p. 20). This process engages students in diagnosing problems; planning, conducting, and critiquing investigations; modeling construction; and communicating data and findings (Linn, Clark, & Slotta, 2003). The American Association for the Advancement of Science (AAAS; 1993) advanced that this approach reflects a "new vision" of active learning that targets scientific process and knowledge.

The NRC (1996) distinguished between inquiry as an instructional approach and inquiry as a set of instructional outcomes. Inquiry as a set of outcomes was further differentiated as "abilities necessary to do scientific inquiry" and "understandings about scientific inquiry" (Olson & Loucks-Horsley, 2000). In their caution against narrow conceptions and enactment of inquiry, Olson and Loucks-Horsley conceptualized enactment of inquiry on a continuum, ensuring fidelity to the essential features of authentic inquiry.

So this provides opportunities for teachers' conceptions of inquiry and enactment of inquiry to improve and evolve with support and guidance over time. It is this practice in all its complexity that we attempt to emulate in school science classrooms.

The Next Generation Science Standards (NGSS; NGSS Lead States, 2013) highlight three dimensions of learning, including practices, crosscutting concepts, and disciplinary core ideas and suggest that science education should "cultivate students' scientific habits of mind, develop their capability to engage in scientific inquiry and teach them how to reason in a scientific context" (p. 41).

These dimensions add a layer of support to understand how scientists conduct scientific research, how knowledge is developed, and how scientific understanding evolves. As such, the NGSS framework provides guidance to contextualize how teachers may interpret science inquiry practices.

Studies have attributed differences in inquiry conceptions and enactment to science disciplinary differences (e.g., Breslyn & McGinnis, 2011) and students' capabilities and understandings of the nature of science (e.g., Lotter, Harwood, & Bonner, 2007). Breslyn and McGinnis (2011) reported that teachers from different subdisciplines held differing conceptions and enactments of inquiry. Whereas biology and earth science teachers approached inquiry as *students conducting scientific investigations* (SCSI), chemistry teachers emphasized *science content knowledge* and SCSI, and physics teachers focused on *modeling*.

The researchers attributed these differences in science teaching to the variations in the structures of the subdisciplines as well as to the context of practice (e.g., curriculum, student ability). Lotter et al. (2007) attributed limited enactment of inquiry to teachers' understandings of the nature of science, so teachers' views of science as a static body of knowledge resulted in traditional orientations to science.

Enactment of inquiry should move beyond an emphasis on habits of mind and conceptual development. Teacher education and professional-development endeavors should explicitly address disciplinary differences and, within these differences, examine how teachers perceive students' abilities, how they understand what science is, and how the context of schooling factors into their decisions about inquiry instruction (e.g., Grossman & Stodolsky, 1995; Mayr, 2004).

INTERACTIONS OF SCIENCE, HISTORY, AND TECHNOLOGY

Although there are many similarities in mathematics and science teacher education, one difference is the sociocultural dimension, which entails teachers knowing how scientific knowledge applies and relates to society. The role of technology in society functions as part of this sociocultural interaction (DeBoer, 1991) and as such should be an essential goal of science education (Bybee & DeBoer, 1994).

Science education reformers, researchers, and educators argue that technology functions as a natural extension to inquiry-based approaches (Aikenhead, 2000). The expectation is that technologies should be part of science instruction, and thus the task of integrating technologies is relegated to science teachers. The NRC (2011) notes that technology is an application of science and its function is to facilitate understandings of the role of science. In this context technology is defined as "all types of human made systems and processes" (pp. 1–4).

This understanding of technology moves beyond limited perspectives that associate technology with electronics and gadgets that make life easier. This perspective is significant because it is customary to focus on technology as *artefact* and overlook the role of technology as *process* (Waight & Abd-El-Khalick, 2012). Understandings of technology as artefact and process illustrate more accurately the complexity of technology integration in the practice of science teaching.

Wahlstrom, Louis, Leithwood, and Anderson (2010) confirmed that teachers are the most important agents in ensuring the success of instruction and innovative approaches. Although this claim is not new, it revisits the responsibilities and expectations that teachers must fulfill as part of their core practice.

For technological enactment, in addition to "understand[ing] their students' needs and conform[ing] the curriculum to the day-to-day realities of their particular school and classroom" (Squire, MaKinster, Barnett, Luehmann, & Barab, 2003, p. 471), teachers must also navigate the unstable nature of technologies and associated knowledge. Teachers' goals and practice (Crawford, 2000) and their prior experience with technology and classroom cultures (Squire et al., 2003) influence how they enact their teaching and how students respond to technologies in instructional environments.

Technology-Supported Inquiry-Based Approaches

So how do we help teachers reconceptualize innovative curriculum and pedagogies in the science classroom? Currently, teacher education focuses on bringing teachers up to speed by emphasizing approaches and skills specific to various software and hardware. One path to technology introduction has occurred via preservice methods courses (Bell & Trundle, 2008; Crawford, Zembal-Saul, Munford, & Friedrichsen, 2005) using inquiry-based approaches to improve students' understandings of scientific concepts (e.g., lunar concepts).

Studies emphasize that technology skills alone were not sustainable. In short, "[t]eaching technology skills alone does little to help teachers develop knowledge about how to use digital tools to teach more effectively" (Koehler & Mishra, 2008, p. 21).

More recently, conversations have shifted to address the pedagogical implications of technology implementation in the science classroom. Technology-supported inquiry requires a repertoire of skills and instructional approaches to effectively enact innovative practices. One such example is the combined emphasis on the interactions of technological, pedagogical content knowledge (TPCK).

The TPCK framework delineates the necessary knowledge components required for successful implementation of technologies in the classroom (American Association of Colleges for Teacher Education [AACTE], 2008). These components include interactions of pedagogical content knowledge, technological content knowledge, and technological pedagogical knowledge.

This framework addresses many important aspects of teaching and learning; however, it also exposes the tremendous expectations placed on teachers. Teachers are required to attend to aspects of content, pedagogical approaches, and knowledge of associated technologies, and at the same time being mindful of student and classroom dynamics.

Koehler and Mishra (2008) remind us that "teaching with technology is a difficult thing to do well" (p. 20) and reconfiguring pedagogy to accommodate technological tools is a rather messy problem. As is evident in the science education literature, researchers, teacher educators, and teachers continue to wrestle with this issue.

Reconsidering Technology: How We Understand the Nature of Technology

The preceding discussion accentuates the complexity of technology-supported inquiry-based approaches; this kind of practice is a multilayered and multifaceted approach that has significant pedagogical implications. In light of the consistent challenges with adoption, implementation, and enactment, we ponder if there are aspects of inquiry or technology that remain unexamined.

Writings on the philosophy of technology (e.g., Arthur, 2009; Pacey, 1983; Tenner, 1996) suggest that understandings of the nature of technology (NoT) provide the most comprehensive understandings of how technology interacts, impacts, and is impacted by society, culture, the economy, and politics. Essentially, this understanding exposes how multiple facets impact how technology manifests in context, including in the science classroom.

Examination of the inherent NoT reveals that the current approaches in the adoption and implementation of technologies in science education remain incomplete (Waight & Abd-El-Khalick, 2012). NoT expands our theoretical lenses to evaluate other dimensions of technology, including notions of culture and values, technological progress, technology as part of systems, technology as a fix, and notions of expertise (see Moore-Russo & Waight, 2015).

Collectively, these dimensions highlight how the classroom functions as a microcosm of the larger society and is governed by historical dimensions, the process and activity of developing technologies, the underlying characteristics of these tools, and the character of the developers and users (Volti, 2010).

In addition, the inherent NoT also brings to prominence the importance of the multiple layers of interactions and impact of technologies on developers and users vis-à-vis the impact of users on technologies in the context of science education.

The role of culture and values helps us understand the inherent NoT. Technology impacts and is impacted by human interactions and thus functions as a culturally viable entity. Science classrooms as cultural entities are also governed by beliefs about students, science, and science teaching that determine how technologies are enacted.

The latter is notable when we consider that most of the technologies that enter the science classroom are either imported from an external context or designed to represent tools used in other professional endeavors (e.g., scientific research). The result is transference of beliefs, values, expertise, principles, and techniques (Volti, 2010) that adds more layers of complexity in classroom dynamics.

The second dimension, the role of expertise in transference and development of technologies, also plays a crucial role in determining the successful use of technology in classrooms. Technologies by nature are unstable and dynamic and thus associated knowledge and skills that govern purpose and use are in constant flux. As such, realizations of technological tools (Bruce & Hogan, 1998; Waight & Abd-El-Khalick, 2007) follow a continuum that is associated with teacher expertise and technological knowledge. The changing nature of these tools has implications for classrooms that function as stable cultural entities.

Although the impetus for technology integration in classrooms is based on perceptions of technological progression, the philosophy of technology cautions how mainstream ideas of progression are often viewed from a linear lens and are misguided and inaccurate. Indeed, using analysis of medical and transportation technologies, philosophers have illustrated how ideas of progression are uniquely human and often rooted in understandings of selective parameters. So, when educators and researchers argue the value of technologies, they do so using data and comparisons from an external culture.

Without regard for cultural context variations, euphoric ideas of advancement may omit other complex interactions that science and mathematics classrooms may not be prepared to address. This array of interactions introduces how technologies as systems function as part of other systems. So to have a complete understanding, one must be able to examine the multiple layers that define technological tools. Explanations in science education that treat only surface features of tools—*procedural guides of what the tool can do*—omit important factors that guide expectations of teachers' practice.

Implications for Technology-Supported Inquiry-Based Practice

Understanding both the potential and boundaries defined by cultural dynamics serves as one of the first steps in negotiating realistic expectations of classroom practice and enactment. In addition to using benchmarks of scientific practice, it is important to outline existing aspects of classroom practice that are malleable and amenable to modifications. For example, the kinds of activities and expertise of teachers and the NoT knowledge should be identified. Benchmarks that define expected outcomes should be rooted in realistic measures of practices that are signature to classroom science.

As noted by Breslyn and McGinnis (2011), disciplinary differences may also play a role. Cognizance of background content knowledge held by teachers and students is related to the preceding discussion. Research has shown that lack of adequate content understanding poses numerous impediments to higher-order habits of mind of inquiry-based approaches. Evaluating the scope of teacher and student content knowledge could help us set more realistic inquiry benchmarks.

CONCLUSION

An irony in science and mathematics education is that most teachers have never experienced what it means to work in their disciplines outside of K–16 education. Yet, it is their connection with, and sense of obligation to, their disciplines that are most likely to prompt instructional modifications.

If teachers come to view the disciplines of mathematics and science as more than transmittable bodies of knowledge, this could lead to changes in what they deem as valid representations in the tasks they assign students and in the ideas and attitudes they foster in students. If teacher educators capitalize on the disciplinary obligation, they stand to influence the beliefs held by teachers and could feasibly break the self-perpetuating cycle of practical rationality that drives mathematics teaching, science teaching, and the use of technology in the classroom.

The discussion outlined herein thus offers a framework to evaluate and revise current expectations of practice. The discussion functions as an alternative pathway to negotiate cultural contexts of science-classroom dynamics and expectations of technological enactment and authentic practice.

If we begin by honoring teachers' context of teaching and learning, it is possible that we may be able to help them understand how innovative approaches are rooted in the kinds of practices they already do. In lieu of NoT, we are reminded that the best understandings of enactment occur within context and associated beliefs and attitudes (Volti, 2010). There is an opportunity here for teachers to engage more critically with the sum components of their practice.

REFERENCES

Aikenhead, G. (2000). Renegotiating the culture of school science. In R. Millar, J. Leach, & J. Osborne (Eds.), *Improving science education: The contributions of research* (246-264). Philadelphia, PA: Open University Press.

American Association of Colleges for Teacher Education. (2008). *Handbook of technological pedagogical content knowledge (TPCK) for educators*. New York: Routledge.

American Association for the Advancement of Science. (1993). *Science for all Americans*. New York: Oxford University Press.

Arthur, W. B. (2009). *The nature of technology*. New York: Free Press.

Ball, D. L. (1988). *Knowledge and reasoning in mathematical pedagogy: Examining what prospective teachers bring to teacher education* (unpublished doctoral dissertation). Michigan State University, East Lansing, MI.

Bell, R. L., & Trundle, K. C. (2008). The use of a computer simulation to promote scientific conceptions of moon phases. *Journal of Research in Science Teaching, 45*, 346-372.

Block, J., & Hazelip, K. (1995). Teachers' beliefs and belief systems. In L. Anderson (Ed.), *International encyclopedia of teaching and teacher education* (2nd ed.; pp. 25-28). Oxford, UK: Elsevier Science Ltd.

Breslyn, W., & McGinnis, J. R. (2011). A comparison of exemplary biology, chemistry, earth science and physics teachers' conceptions and enactment of inquiry. *Science Education, 96*, 48-77.

Bruce, B. C., & Hogan, M. P. (1998). The disappearance of technology: Towards an ecological model of literacy. In D. Reinking, M. McKenna, L. D. Labbo, & R. D. Kieffer (Eds.), *Handbook of literacy and technology: Transformations in a post-typographic world* (pp. 269-281). Mahwah, NJ: Lawrence Erlbaum.

Bourdieu, P. (1998). *Practical Reason*. Palo Alto, CA: Stanford University Press.

Bybee, R. W., & DeBoer, G. E. (1994). Research on goals for the science curriculum. In D. L. Gabel (Ed.), *Handbook of research on science teaching and learning* (pp. 357-387). New York, NY: Macmillan.

Chazan, D., Sela, H., & Herbst, P. (2012). Is the role of equations in the doing of word problems in school algebra changing? Initial indications from teacher study groups. *Cognition and Instruction, 30*(1), 1-38.

Cobb, P., Boufi, A., McClain, K., & Whitenack, J. (1997). Reflexive discourse and collective reflection. *Journal of Research in Mathematics Education, 28*, 258-277.

Cobb, P., Yackel, E., & Wood, T. (1992). A constructivist alternative to the representational view of mind in mathematics education. *Journal for Research in Mathematics Education, 23*, 2-33.

Cohen, D., Raudenbush, S., & Ball, D. (2003). Resources, instruction, and research. *Educational Evaluation and Policy Analysis, 25*, 119–142.

Crawford, B. A. (2000). Embracing the essence of inquiry: New roles for science teachers. *Journal of Research in Science Teaching, 37*, 916–937.

Crawford, B. A., Zembal-Saul, C., Munford, D., & Friedrichsen, P. (2005). Confronting prospective teachers' ideas of evolution and scientific inquiry using technology and inquiry-based tasks. *Journal of Research in Science Teaching, 42*, 613–637.

Cross, D. I. (2009). Alignment, cohesion, and change: examining mathematics teachers' belief structures and their influence on instructional practices. *Journal of Mathematics Teacher Education, 12*(5), 325–346.

Cuoco, A., Goldenberg, E. P., & Mark, J. (1996). Habits of mind: An organizing principle for mathematics curricula. *The Journal of Mathematical Behavior, 15*(4), 375–402.

DeBoer, G. E. (1991). *A history of ideas in science education: Implications for practice*. New York, NY: Teachers College Press.

De Villiers, M. (1998). To teach definitions in geometry or teach to define? In A. Olivier and K. Newstead (Eds.), *Proceedings of the 22nd international conference for the psychology of mathematics education* (vol. 2; pp. 248–255). Stellenbosch, South Africa: University of Stellenbosch.

Eiriksson, S. (1997). Preservice teachers' perceived constraints of teaching science in the elementary classroom. *Journal of Elementary Science Education, 9*(2), 18–27.

Feiman-Nemser, S., & Buchmann, M. (1987). When is student teaching teacher education? *Teaching and Teacher Education, 3*, 255–273.

Fosnot, C. (1989). *Enquiring teachers, enquiring learners: a constructivist approach to teaching*. New York: Teachers College Press.

Gallagher, J. J. (2007). *Teaching science for understanding: A practical guide for middle and high school teachers*. Upper Saddle River, NJ: Pearson Education, Inc.

Grossman, P., & McDonald, M. (2008). Back to the future: Directions for research in teaching and teacher education. *American Educational Research Journal, 45*(1), 184–205.

Grossman, P. L., & Stodolsky, S. S. (1995). Content as context: The role of school subjects in secondary school teaching. *Educational Researcher, 24*, 5–23.

Handal, B. (2003). Teachers' mathematics beliefs: A review. *The Mathematics Educator, 13*(2), 47–57.

Herbst, P., & Balacheff, N. (2009). Proving and knowing in public: The nature of proof in a classroom. In M. Blanton, D. Stylianou, & E. Knuth (Eds.), *The teaching and learning of proof across the grades: A K–16 perspective* (pp. 40–64). Mahwah, NJ: Routledge.

Herbst, P., & Chazan, D. (2003). Exploring the practical rationality of mathematics teaching through conversations about videotaped episodes: the case of engaging students in proving. *For the Learning of Mathematics, 23*(1), 2–14.

Herbst, P., & Chazan, D. (2011). Research on practical rationality: Studying the justification of actions in mathematics teaching. *The Mathematics Enthusiast, 8*, 405–462.

Hewson, P. W., & Hewson, M. G. (1988). An appropriate conception of teaching science: A view from studies of science learning. *Science Education, 72*, 597–614.

Kagan, D. (1992). Implications of research on teacher belief. *Educational Psychologist, 27*(1), 65–90.

Kieran, C. (2013). The false dichotomy in mathematics education between conceptual understanding and procedural skills: An example from algebra. In K. R. Leathem (Ed.), *Vital directions for mathematics education research* (pp. 153–171). New York: Springer.

Koballa, T., Graber, W., Coleman, D. C., & Kemp, A. C. (2000). Prospective gymnasium teachers' conceptions of chemistry learning and teaching. *International Journal of Science Education, 22*, 209–224.

Koehler, M. J., & Mishra, P. (2008). Introducing TPCK. In AACTE (Eds.), *Handbook of technological pedagogical content knowledge (TPCK) for Educators* (pp. 3–29). New York: Routledge.

Lave, J., & Wenger, E. (1991). *Situated learning: Legitimate peripheral participation*. Cambridge, UK: Cambridge University Press.

Leikin, R., & Winicki-Landman, G. (2001). Defining as a vehicle for professional development of secondary school mathematics teachers. *Mathematics Education Research Journal, 3*, 62–73.

Liljedahl, P. (2005). Mathematical discovery and *affect*: The *effect* of AHA! experiences on undergraduate mathematics students. *International Journal of Mathematical Education In Science and Technology, 36*(2–3), 219–234.

Liljedahl, P. (2008). Teachers' insights into the relationship between beliefs and practice. In J. Maab and W. Schloglmann (Eds.), *Beliefs and attitudes in mathematics education: New research results* (pp. 33–44). Rotterdam, Netherlands: Sense Publishers.

Liljedahl, P., Chernoff, E., & Zazkis, R. (2007). Interweaving mathematics and pedagogy in task design: A tale of one task. *Journal of Mathematics Teacher Education, 10*, 239–249.

Liljedahl, P., Rolka, K., & Rösken, B. (2007). Affecting affect: The reeducation of preservice teachers' beliefs about mathematics and mathematics teaching and learning. In W. G. Martin, M. E. Strutchens, & P. C. Elliott (Eds.), *The learning of mathematics. sixty-ninth yearbook of the national council of teachers of mathematics* (pp. 319–330). Reston, VA: NCTM.

Linn, M. C., Clark, D., & Slotta, J. D. (2003). WISE design for knowledge integration. *Science Education, 87*, 517–538.

Lortie, D. (1975). *Schoolteacher: A sociological study*. Chicago, IL: University of Chicago Press.

Lotter, C., Harwood, W. S., & Bonner, J. (2007). The influence of core teaching conceptions on teachers' use of inquiry teaching practices. *Journal of Research in Science Teaching, 44*, 1318–1347.

Mathews, M. R. (1998). In defense of modest goals when teaching about the nature of science. *Journal of Research in Science Teaching, 35*(2), 161–174.

Mayr, E. (2004). *What makes biology unique? Considerations on the autonomy of a scientific discipline*. Cambridge, UK: Cambridge University Press.

Millsaps, G. (2000). Secondary mathematics teachers' mathematics autobiographies: Definitions of mathematics and beliefs about mathematics instructional practice. *Focus on Learning Problems in Mathematics, 22*(1), 45–67.

Moore-Russo, D. (2010). A critique and reaction to practical rationality as a framework for mathematics teaching. In P. Brosnan, D. B. Erchick, & L. Flevares (Eds.), *Proceedings of the 32nd annual meeting of the North American chapter of the international group for the psychology of mathematics education.* (vol. 6; pp. 55–59). Columbus: Ohio State University.

Moore-Russo, D., & Waight, N. (2015). Rethinking how mathematics, science and technology are represented in teacher education. *Teacher Education and Practice, 28*(2/3), 221–238.

Moore-Russo, D., & Weiss, M. (2011). Practical rationality, the disciplinary obligation, and authentic mathematical work: A look at geometry. *The Mathematics Enthusiast, 8*(3), 463–482.

National Council of Teachers of Mathematics. (1989). *Curriculum and evaluation standards for school mathematics.* Reston, VA: Author.

National Council of Teachers of Mathematics. (2000). *Principles and standards for school mathematics.* Reston, VA: Author.

National Council of Teachers of Mathematics. (2006). *Curriculum focal points for prekindergarten through grade 8 mathematics: A quest for coherence.* Reston, VA: Author.

National Governors Association for Best Practices and Council of Chief State School Officers. (2010). *Common Core state standards mathematics.* Washington, DC: Author.

National Research Council (NRC). (1996). *National science education standards.* Washington, DC: National Academy Press.

National Research Council (NRC). (2001). *Adding it up: Helping children learn mathematics.* Washington, DC: National Academy Press.

National Research Council (NRC). (2011). *A framework for K–12 science education: Practices, crosscutting concepts, and core ideas.* Washington, DC: National Academy Press.

NGSS Lead States. (2013). *Next generation science standards: For states, by states.* Washington, DC: National Academies Press.

Olson, S., & Loucks-Horsley, S. (Eds.). (2000). *Inquiry and the national science education standards: A Guide for teaching and learning.* Washington, DC: National Academy Press.

Pacey, A. (1983). *The culture of technology.* Cambridge, MA: MIT Press.

Pajares, M. (1992). Teachers' beliefs and educational research: Cleaning up a messy construct. *Review of Educational Research, 62,* 307–332.

Phelps, A. J., & Lee, C. (2003). The power of practice: What students learn from how we teach. *Journal of Chemical Education, 80,* 829–832.

Popkewitz, T. S. (2000). The denial of change in educational change: Systems of ideas in the construction of national policy and evaluation. *Educational Researcher, 29,* 17–19.

Renzaglia, A., Hutchins, M., & Lee, S. (1997). The impact of teacher education on the beliefs, attitudes, and dispositions of preservice special educations. *Teacher Education and Special Education, 4*, 360–377.

Selling, S. K., Garcia, N., & Ball, D. L. (2016). What does it take to develop assessments of mathematical knowledge for teaching? Unpacking the mathematical work of teaching. *The Mathematics Enthusiast, 13*(1/2), 35.

Silver, E. A. (1994). On mathematical problem posing. *For the Learning of Mathematics, 14*(1), 19–28.

Silverman, J., & Thompson, P. W. (2008). Toward a framework for the development of mathematical knowledge for teaching. *Journal of Mathematics Teacher Education, 11*, 499–511.

Squire, K. D., Makinster, J. G., Barnett, M., Luehmann, A. L., & Barab, S. L. (2003). Designed curriculum and local culture: Acknowledging the primacy of classroom culture. *Science Education, 87*, 468–489.

Skott, J. (2001). The emerging practices of a novice teacher: The roles of his school mathematics images. *Journal of Mathematics Teacher Education, 4*, 3–28.

Skott, J. (2009). 'Contextualising the notion of belief enactment.' *Journal of Mathematics Teacher Education, 12*, 27–46.

Stinner, A. (1992) Science textbooks and science teaching: From logic to evidence. *Science Education*, 76, 1–16.

Tenner, E. (1996). *Why things bite back: Technology and the revenge of unintended consequences*. New York: First Vintage Books Edition.

Thompson, A. G. (1985). Teachers' conceptions of mathematics and the teaching of problem solving. In E. A. Silver (Ed.), *Teaching and learning mathematical problem solving: Multiple research perspectives* (pp. 281–294). Hillsdale, NJ: Erlbaum.

Thompson, A. G. (1992). Teachers' beliefs and conceptions: A synthesis of the research. In D. A. Grouws (Ed.), *Handbook of research on mathematics teaching and learning* (pp. 189–236). Hillsdale, NJ: Erlbaum.

Thompson, P. W. (2008). Conceptual analysis of mathematics ideas: Some spadework at the foundation of mathematics education. In O. Figueras, J. L. Cortina, S. Alatorre, T. Rojano, & A. Sépulveda (Eds.), *Proceedings of the joint meeting of international group for the psychology of mathematics education and the north American group for the psychology of mathematics education* (vol. 1; pp. 45–64). Morélia, Mexico: PME.

Törner, G., Rolka, K., Roesken, B., & Sriraman, B. (2010). Understanding a teacher's actions in the classroom by applying Schoenfeld's theory teaching-in-context. In B. Sriraman and L. English (Eds.), *Theories of mathematics education: Seeking new frontiers* (pp. 401–417). New York, NY: Springer.

Volti, R. (2010). *Society and Technological Change*. New York: Worth Publishers.

Von Glasersfeld, E. (1987). Learning as a constructive activity. In C. Janvier (Ed.), *Problems of representation in the teaching and learning of mathematics* (pp. 3–17). Hillsdale, NJ: Lawrence Erlbaum Associates.

Wahlstrom, K. L., Louis, K. S., Leithwood, K., & Anderson, S. E. (2010). *Investigating the links to improved student learning: Executive summary of research findings*.

Minneapolis, MN: Center for Applied Research and Educational Improvement, University of Minnesota.

Waight, N., & Abd-El-Khalick, F. (2007). The Impact of technology on the enactment of inquiry in a technology enthusiast's sixth grade science classroom. *Journal of Research in Science Teaching, 44,* 154–182.

Waight, N., & Abd-El-Khalick, F. (2011). From scientific practice to high school science: Transfer of scientific technologies and realizations of authentic inquiry. *Journal of Research In Science Teaching, 48,* 37–70.

Waight, N., & Abd-El-Khalick, F. (2012). Nature of technology: Implications for design, development, and enactment of technological tools in school science classrooms. *International Journal of Science Education, 34,* 2875–28905.

Weiss, M. K. (2009). *Mathematical sense, mathematical sensibility: The role of the secondary geometry course in teaching students to be like mathematicians* (Doctoral Dissertation). Retrieved from *Dissertation Abstracts International, 71*(2). (UMI No. 3392784).

Weiss, M., & Moore-Russo, D. (2012). Thinking like a mathematician. *Mathematics Teacher, 106*(4), 269–273.

Weiss, M., Herbst, P., & Chen, C. (2009). Teachers' perspectives on mathematical proof and the two-column form. *Educational Studies in Mathematics, 70,* 275–293.

Wenger, E. (1998). *Communities of practice: Learning, meaning, and identity.* New York: Cambridge University Press.

Wiggins, G., & Mctighe, J. (2005). *Understanding by design.* Alexandria, VA: Association for Supervision and Curriculum Development.

Wilson, S., & Cooney, T. (2002). Mathematics teacher change and development. In G. C. Leder, E. Pehkonen, & G. Törner (Eds.), *Beliefs: A hidden variable in mathematics education?* (pp. 127–147). Dordrecht, Netherlands: Kluwer Academic Publishers.

Yackel, E., & Cobb, P. (1996). Sociomathematical norms, argumentation, and autonomy in mathematics. *Journal for Research in Mathematics Education, 27,* 458–477.

Yerrick, R., Radosta, M., & Greene, K. (2018). Technology, Culture, and Young Science Teachers: A Promise Unfulfilled and Proposals for Change. In Y. Dori, Z. Mevarech, & D. Baker (Eds.), *Cognition, metacognition, and culture in STEM education. Innovations in science education and technology* (vol. 24; pp. 117–138). Cham, Switzerland: Springer.

Part II

Complexities and Challenges in STEM Education

The complex and challenging problems that we currently face are the driving force behind national calls for changes in science, technology, engineering, and math (STEM) education (National Center on Education and the Economy, 2007; National Research Council [NRC], 2011, 2012; National Science Learning Centre, 2013).

One of the major problems confronting STEM education lies in the realization that although educators are aware of the importance of STEM education, neither teacher educators nor researchers consistently agree on or understand what STEM teachers should know or how STEM teachers should be prepared for teaching STEM in K–12 education. Currently, STEM disciplines are taught in silos, which is an equally important problem that requires attention.

Interestingly, the nature of responsibilities that define the work that STEM workforce professionals do each day blurs the lines between disciplines; the STEM workforce advances an important understanding of the interdisciplinary nature of STEM. Preparing teachers in an interdisciplinary approach would be more in line with the nature of work associated with STEM professionals.

One of the greater educational challenges for interdisciplinary STEM education is that few general guidelines or models exist for teacher educators to follow regarding how to prepare STEM teachers using STEM-integration approaches in their classroom (Bybee, 2013; Johnson, Monk, & Swain, 2000; Wang, Moore, Roehrig, & Park, 2011).

STEM education is not without its complexities and challenges nor is STEM teacher preparation. Klein (2005), writing on the nature of interdisciplinarity and the dynamics of collaboration and integration across disciplines, delineated the complexity of STEM by highlighting some key constructs, such as organizational structure, task responsibilities, integrative activities, interdisciplinary perspectives, and pedagogical and content knowledge.

Because interdisciplinary teacher preparation transcends the boundaries of disciplines, the perception of the organizational structure of STEM is extremely complex. How STEM "knowledge is defined and disseminated; how and what students learn; and how higher education can be responsive to its external environment are crucial issues facing educators" (Holley, 2017, p. 1).

STEM education not withstanding, the complexities of today's world require all people to be equipped with a new set of core knowledge and skills to solve ever-more complex and difficult problems, design new and more advanced ways of addressing the needs of a changing society, gather and evaluate evidence, and make sense of information they receive from varied sources. In turn, what is required are new interdisciplinary approaches to STEM teacher preparation that translate into STEM education in K–12 schools.

Bailey, Kaufman, and Subotic (2015), Betrus (2015), Dweck, Walton, and Cohen (2014), and Sharples (2000) acknowledged that the learning and doing of STEM provides pathways to develop the knowledge and skills necessary to not only meeting the challenges we face today but also in preparing new solutions for problems yet to be experienced. Equally important, STEM education advances new knowledges and skills necessary to preparing students for a future where current knowledge and skills may not be sufficient.

Baker-Doylea and Yoonb (2011) explained that the dynamic nature and complexity of STEM disciplines make professional development a challenging task. This becomes more evident when considering the complexity of interdisciplinary STEM education and teacher preparation. This complexity exists on multiple levels: between the different STEM and non-STEM disciplines, between different fields of study, between different research agendas, between institutional and academic cultures, and between the work and structure perceived to be normative for higher education in general and teacher preparation in particular (see Holley, 2017).

Preparing interdisciplinary STEM teachers, pedagogically, is not synonymous with a single process, set of skills, method, or technique. Instead, interdisciplinary pedagogy is concerned primarily with fostering a sense of self-authorship and a situated, partial, and perspectival notion of knowledge that teachers can use to respond to complex questions, issues, or problems, while designing place-based activities that situate the preservice teacher–candidate in experiential learning situations that cultivate optimal epistemological understandings of what knowledges are needed to solve complex problems.

Haynes (2002) has argued the point that the interdisciplinary approach to STEM teacher preparation "necessarily entails the cultivation of the many cognitive skills such as differentiating, reconciling, and synthesizing . . . it also involves promotion of student's interpersonal and intrapersonal learning" (p. xvi).

Given the complexities and challenges that we face in the present and portend for the future, we require an interdisciplinary approach to teacher preparation that cultivates in those teachers new conceptual structures aligned with interdisciplinary STEM education. A major challenge will be to develop integrated STEM curriculum, a process that is complex and challenging because integration of subjects is more than a matter of simply putting different subject areas together. Rather, integration of STEM curriculum that advances an interdisciplinary approach to teaching and learning will require an awareness and understanding that real-world problems are not separated into isolated disciplines.

There are external and internal factors that directly affect STEM teacher preparation. Whether cultural, political, or epistemological in nature, these factors present challenges that must be addressed in preparing a future generation of STEM teachers to enter K–12 schools and classrooms.

Similarly, there are interactions between the external and internal constraints that negatively influenced teacher educators' STEM pedagogical approaches to preparing those teachers. In many cases, external factors interact with internal constraints related to STEM teacher educators' pedagogical content knowledge (PCK), including the lack of pedagogical knowledge about STEM, the lack of mathematics, technology, and engineering knowledge, and perhaps most importantly, an understanding of the need for and knowledge of how to create an interdisciplinary approach to teacher preparation.

The problem of external and internal factors as well as the constraints is noted as key areas of concern by researchers (EL-Deghaidy, 2006; Mansour, 2007, 2010, 2013; Mansour, EL-Deghaidy, Al-Shamrani, & Aldahmash, 2014; Johnson et al., 2000). The factors and constraints are cyclical as well as multifaceted, presenting complex and often ill-defined problems that act as mediating factors against new approaches to STEM education and an interdisciplinary approach to teacher preparation.

REFERENCES

Bailey, A., Kaufman, E., & Subotic, S. (2015). *Education, technology, and the twenty-first-century skills gap.* Retrieved November 27, 2018, from https://www.bcg.com/en-us/publications/2015/public-sector-education-technology-21st-century-skill-gap.aspx.

Baker-Doylea, K., & Yoonb, S. (2011). In search of practitioner-based social capital: A social network analysis tool for understanding and facilitating teacher collaboration in a US-based STEM professional development program. *Professional Development in Education, 37*(1), 75–93.

Betrus, A. (2015). *Through STEM education our future is bright.* Retrieved November 27, 2018, from http://www.fourthcoastentertainment.com/story/2015/08/01/entertainment/through-stem-education-our-future-is-bright/242.html.

Bybee, R. (2013). *The case for STEM education: Challenges and opportunities.* Arlington, VA: National Science Teachers Association Press.

Dweck, C. S., Walton, G. M., & Cohen, G. L. (2014). *Mindsets and skills that promote long-term learning.* Seattle, WA: Bill and Melinda Gates Foundation.

EL-Deghaidy, H. (2006). An investigation of pre-service teacher's self-efficacy and self-image as a science teacher in Egypt. *Asia-pacific forum on science learning and teaching.* Retrieved November 27, 2018, from https://www.ied.edu.hk/apfslt/v7_issue2/heba/.

Haynes, C. (2002). Introduction: Laying a foundation for interdisciplinary teaching. In C. Haynes (Ed.), *Innovations in interdisciplinary teaching* (pp. xi–xxii). Washington, DC: American Council on Education/Oryx Press.

Holley, K. (2017). Interdisciplinary curriculum and learning in higher education. In *Oxford research encyclopedia of education.* Retrieved from http://education.oxfordre.com/view/10.1093/acrefore/9780190264093.001.0001/acrefore-9780190264093-e-138.

Johnson, S., Monk, M., & Swain, J. (2000). Constraints on development and change to science teachers' practice in Egyptian classrooms. *Journal of Education for Teaching, 26*(1), 9–24.

Klein, J. T. (2005). Interdisciplinary teamwork: The dynamics of collaboration and integration. In S. J. Derry, C. D. Schunn, & M. A. Gernsbacher (Eds.), *Interdisciplinary Collaboration: An emerging cognitive science* (pp. 23–50). Mahwah, NJ: Lawrence Erlbaum.

Mansour, N. (2007). Challenges to STS Education: Implications for Science Teacher Education. *Bulletin of Science, Technology and Society, 27*(6), 482–497. doi:10.1177/0270467607308286.

Mansour, N. (2010). The impact of the knowledge and beliefs of egyptian science teachers in integrating an STS based curriculum. *Journal of Science Teacher Education, 21*(5), 513–534. Doi:10.1007/S10972- 010-9193-0.

Mansour, N. (2013). Consistencies and inconsistencies between science teachers' beliefs and practices. *International Journal of Science Education, 35*(7), 1230–1275. doi:10.1080/09500693.2012.743196.

Mansour, N., EL-Deghaidy, H., Al-Shamrani, S., & Aldahmash, A. (2014). Rethinking the theory and practice of continuing professional development: Science teachers' perspectives. *Research in Science Education, 44* (6), 949–973.

National Center on Education and the Economy. (2007). *Tough choices or tough times: The report of the New Commission on the Skills of the American Workforce.* San Francisco: Wiley.

National Research Council (NRC). (2011). *Successful K–12 STEM education: Identifying effective approaches in science, technology, engineering, and mathematics.* Committee on Highly Successful Science Programs for K–12 Science Education.

Board on Science Education and Board on Testing and Assessment, Division of Behavioral and Social Sciences and Education. Washington, DC: The National Academies Press.

National Research Council (NRC). (2012). *A framework for K–12 science education: Practices, crosscutting concepts, and core ideas*. Committee on a Conceptual Framework for New K–12 Science Education Standards. Board on Science Education, Division of Behavioral and Social Sciences and Education. Washington, DC: The National Academies Press.

National Science Learning Centre. (2013). The future of STEM education. White Paper Submitted to The National Science Learning Centre, University of York, New York, July 17, 2013.

Sharples, M. (2000). The design of personal mobile technologies for lifelong learning. *Computers and Education, 34*, 177–193. Retrieved November 27, 2018, from https://www.tlu.ee/~kpata/haridustehnoloogiatlu/technolohiesforlifelong.pdf.

Wang, H., Moore, T., Roehrig, G. H., & Park, M. S. (2011). STEM integration: Teacher perceptions and practice. *Journal of Pre-College Engineering Education Research (J-PEER), 1*(2), 1–13. Retrieved November 27, 2018, from http://dx.doi.org/10.5703/1288284314636.

Chapter 6

Developing a STEM Education Teacher Preparation Program to Help Increase STEM Literacy among Preservice Teachers

Margaret Mohr-Schroeder, Christa Jackson, D. Craig Schroeder, and Jennifer Wilhelm

The twentieth century was characterized as a time when the United States was unparalleled in education and in the production of the world's best scientists, engineers, and mathematicians. Although the more recent worldwide participation in science, technology, engineering, and math (STEM) discoveries and related technologies is of enormous benefit to the global community, the United States' diminishing relative contribution in the STEM disciplines is the cause of significant trepidation based predominantly on the economic impact of the United States losing its competitive and creative edges (see National Academy of Sciences, 2007; Florida, 2005).

In response, there is an ongoing national movement to increase the number of individuals ready to enter the STEM workforce who are well prepared to tackle the most-pressing concerns in science including those in medicine and industry. To meet these ends, various stakeholders are calling on institutions of higher education to increase the number of competent students graduating with STEM-related degrees.

Additionally, realizing that the current lack of qualified science and mathematics teachers in the K–12 system has had a ripple effect in the STEM pipeline, postsecondary institutions are also attempting to increase the number of STEM-certified educators for the secondary level. Increasing the numbers of secondary educators, of course, is not enough, and better teacher preparation is an important accompanying goal.

Currently, many secondary students are not motivated to engage in advanced STEM courses in high school and lack the necessary mathematics and science knowledge to enter and maintain scholarship in those fields beyond the secondary level. The "State Indicators of Science and Mathematics Education" (Council of Chief State School Officers, 2005) report indicates that increases in standards for learning require improved secondary-level teaching of mathematics and science if US students are to compete in twenty-first–century knowledge economies.

The National Academies report *Educating Teachers of Science, Mathematics, and Technology: New Practices for the Millennium* (National Research Council [NRC], 2001) presents several strategies to better address the need for more qualified *and* effective STEM teachers. In brief, these strategies stress the need for collaboration among various stakeholders. This report states that "responsibility for teacher education in science, mathematics, and technology can no longer be delegated only to schools of education and school districts . . . scientists, mathematicians and engineers must become more informed about and involved in this effort" (NRC, 2001, p. xi). Research confirms there is a strong positive relationship among the level of educator course preparation in mathematics and science fields and the level of student achievement (Darling-Hammond, 2000; Fetler, 1999; Monk, 1994).

The lack of highly qualified mathematics and science teachers in middle- and high-school classrooms in the United States is a crisis that is well established. For example, unqualified teachers (i.e., out-of-field teachers) teach about 56 percent of high-school students taking physical science and 27 percent taking mathematics. These percentages are magnified in high-poverty areas. Students enrolled in schools with high minority populations have less than a 50 percent chance of having a science or mathematics teacher who has both a degree and license in the discipline taught (Darling-Hammond, 1999).

Judy Jeffrey, a leader in the National Council of Chief State School Officers and the director of the Iowa State Department of Education, says, "In any given year, I have more openings for physics teachers than I can fill because I can't find highly qualified teachers in this field." This is compounded with the attrition of K–12 teachers.

Over the coming decade, approximately two-thirds of K–12 teachers will either retire or leave the workforce. Of that, about 200,000 are secondary mathematics and science teachers (National Academy of Sciences, 2007). The shortage of science and mathematics teachers is evident in the American Association for Employment in Education (AAEE) 2007 report, *Educator Supply and Demand in the United States* (figure 6.1).

The shortage and lack of qualified mathematics and science teachers has had a detrimental effect on the job market. A US Department of Labor, Employment, and Training Administration report (2007) remarks that three-quarters of students in the United States are not prepared for college studies in

Developing a STEM Education Teacher Preparation Program 95

AAEE Estimates of Relative Demand for Teachers by Subject Area on a Five Point Scale in 2007 (1=Considerable Surplus, 5=Considerable Shortage)

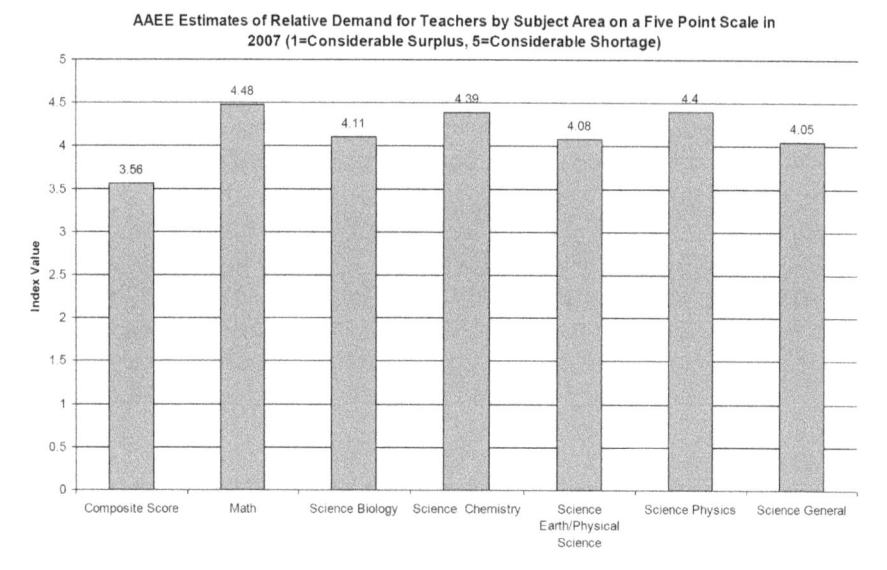

Subject	Index Value
Composite Score	3.56
Math	4.48
Science Biology	4.11
Science Chemistry	4.39
Science Earth/Physical Science	4.08
Science Physics	4.4
Science General	4.05

Figure 6.1 Relative demand for STEM teachers by subject area.
Source: author created.

mathematics, science, engineering, and technology. Furthermore, according to a National Association of Manufacturers survey, 51 percent of employers state their graduates are "deficient in math and science" (Foster, 2010). If the United States is to be a leader in engineering, technology, and innovation in the global market, the state of science and mathematics education must be reversed.

Time and time again, research confirms that investments in teacher preparation pay off. STEM PLUS will dramatically increase the investment of the University of Kentucky (UK) in producing highly qualified and effective secondary STEM educators. Specifically, STEM PLUS aims to produce a network of STEM teachers working in high-need schools who can serve as teacher–leaders that are knowledgeable about the STEM disciplines and able to ensure the success and advanced participation of their diverse students with high needs in STEM disciplines.

The STEM PLUS program is the first program to offer a major in STEM Education. Several programs, including the University of Arizona and UTEACH, have programs that fall under a STEM Education umbrella, but their graduates still receive a degree in their particular area of concentration, and their programs do not necessarily focus on the integration of mathematics and science. We have structured STEM PLUS to engage candidates in more interdisciplinary and transdisciplinary study through a STEM lens.

By focusing the major on STEM Education, STEM PLUS graduates will emerge with a more interdisciplinary foundation, be more knowledgeable about the similarities and differences uniting knowledge across the disciplines, and be more likely to implement interdisciplinary lessons, all the while being just as versed as their peers from traditional programs in terms of disciplinary content knowledge.

In turn, students in the classrooms of STEM PLUS teachers will develop greater understanding of the transdisciplinary and multidisciplinary nature of STEM, a more realistic exposure to actual work in STEM, and ultimately, a more positive experience in their secondary STEM pursuits, which are all factors that research confirms have a direct impact on student academic achievement, interest, and retention in STEM involvement at the postsecondary level.

A TRANSDISCIPLINARY, CLINICAL APPROACH TO STEM TEACHER PREPARATION

The core of STEM PLUS is an innovative transdisciplinary, clinically based undergraduate certification program through which preservice mathematics and science (i.e., biology, chemistry, physical science, physics, and computer science) teachers will earn a double major in their respective content area and in STEM Education. State certification will be earned after the successful completion of the program in the preservice teacher's respective content area.

The STEM PLUS program is unique and innovative in that it is the first program in the United States resulting in a degree and certification that truly prepares teacher candidates as secondary (grades 8–12) STEM specialists, while still ensuring a deep understanding of their certified content area through a discipline major. The coursework for the program consists of four distinct components (table 6.1).

Candidates will earn a Bachelor of Science in STEM Education and their discipline (i.e., mathematics, physics, chemistry, biology, physical science, or computer science) in 120 credit hours over four years. At the successful completion of their program, candidates will be eligible to apply for their Rank III[1] Provisional[2] Certification in their discipline area(s) for grades 8–12. Although one of the candidate's majors will be STEM Education, there is no STEM certification at the state level. STEM Education (the combination of STEM content courses and STEM education courses) is considered an area of concentration, not a discipline, especially at the secondary (grades 8–12) level.

In this program, there is a heavy focus on content knowledge and a focus on methods and researched-based practices in STEM pedagogy. The purpose and focus of the STEM Education courses is to bridge the gap between

Table 6.1 Coursework for STEM PLUS Program

Coursework	Purpose
UK CORE: A 30-hour sequence of general-education courses in which students demonstrate (a) an understanding of and ability to employ the processes of intellectual inquiry within and across four knowledge areas: arts and creativity, humanities, social and behavioral sciences, and natural/physical/mathematical sciences [12 hours]; (b) competent written, oral, and visual communication skills both as producers and consumers of information [6 hours]; (c) an understanding of and ability to employ methods of quantitative reasoning [6 hours]; and (d) an understanding of the complexities of citizenship and the process for making informed choices as engaged citizens in a diverse, multilingual world [6 hours].	To meet the general-education requirements outlined by the university and to ensure well-rounded teacher candidates
STEM Education Major: A transdisciplinary and clinically based major in which candidates are immersed in STEM education coursework, which includes more than 300 hours of focused field experiences	Create STEM knowledge for teaching through project-based instruction, especially in the certification area(s) and with respect to environmental sustainability; to help bridge the gap between pedagogy and content; application to the secondary classroom in terms of securing STEM literacy for all students
Discipline Major: A discipline major in which candidates gain a deep understanding of the content they will teach	Create a depth of content knowledge in the specific STEM discipline in which the candidate will be certified
STEM Support Courses: Candidates will take a variety of STEM coursework outside of their discipline area to broaden their knowledge of STEM. All candidates will be required to take at least one engineering course.	To create a basic understanding of the various STEM disciplines and their interdisciplinary nature and connections; gain content knowledge in additional STEM areas other than certifiable area
TOTAL	**120 hours**

content knowledge and teaching and to foster a rich in-depth knowledge for teachers regarding their particular subject area (Hill, Schilling, & Ball, 2004) within a wider multidisciplinary context. In addition, this coursework and the content coursework defined for the additional certification areas meet the requirements to teach Advanced Placement (AP) courses and International Baccalaureate courses in science and mathematics.

Why a Transdisciplinary Approach?

Since the launch of Sputnik and the passing of the National Defense Education Act of 1958 in its wake (Carney, Chubin, & Malcom, 2008), US governmental and nongovernmental organizations have continued to increase their funding of endeavors meant to improve K–20 STEM education, mostly with the ultimate goal of swelling the pipeline of individuals that will, eventually, grow the national STEM workforce (Carney et al., 2008; Kuenzi, 2008). Other reports, such as *A Nation at Risk* (National Commission on Excellence in Education, 1983) and *Rising above the Gathering Storm* (National Academy of Sciences, 2007), have kept the concern for STEM education reform paramount in the nation's psyche. STEM is more than just a convenient acronym and the wide call for educators prepared to find commonalities while respecting disciplinary differences as they talk and teach across them is loud indeed.

As research has provided a deeper knowledge base among so many disciplines, society has often wrestled with how to integrate that knowledge both on macroscopic and microscopic levels. As our knowledge production continues to increase and we continue to delineate disciplines in our chosen methodology of instruction, we must begin to ask ourselves how we might bridge the apparent gaps between what we know and how we solve problems. Transdisciplinary research and instructional methods have sought to bridge those gaps (Klein, 2008; Romey, 1975).

Moreover, transdisciplinary instruction can be viewed as a viable instructional, research, and institutional approach that can unify varied perspectives from diverse disciplines by bridging knowledge production and solutions to societal problems (Hirsch Hadorn et al., 2008). We define *transdisciplinary* as an emphasis on engagement, investigation, and participation that specifically addresses present-day issues and problems in a way that explicitly destabilizes disciplinary boundaries, while at the same time respecting disciplinary expertise (Klein, Grossenbacher-Mansuy, & Häberli, 2001; Nicolescu, 2002; figure 6.2).

Transdisciplinary STEM Curricula Enacted

Klein (2008) offers that the framework for fully developing a transdisciplinary curriculum is rooted in (1) disciplinary depth, (2) multidisciplinary breadth, (3) interdisciplinary integration, and (4) transdisciplinary competencies. The STEM Plus program uses preservice teachers' established disciplinary depth in their content area to build experiences that translate to transdisciplinary competencies. That is to say, the STEM PLUS program focuses on themes

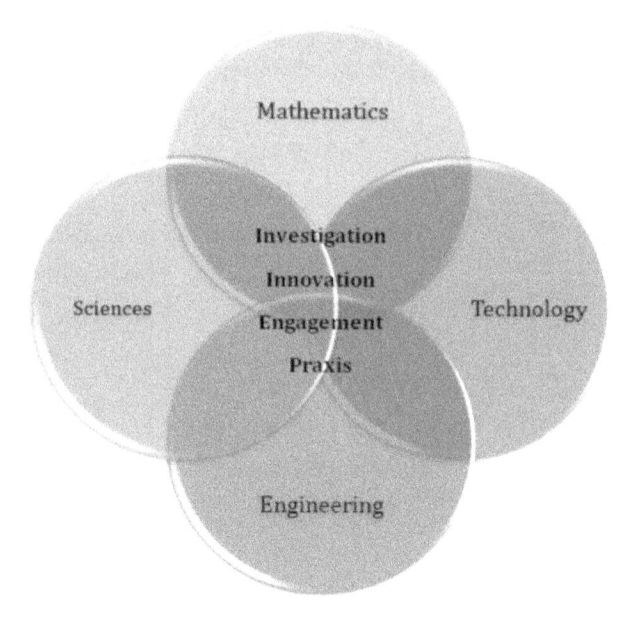

Developing a STEM Education Teacher Preparation Program 99

Figure 6.2 Transdisciplinary approach uniting the University of Kentucky's STEM Education Department endeavors. *Source*: author created.

uniting all of STEM, more specifically, the seven cross-cutting concepts found in *A Framework for the Next Generation Science Standards* (NGSS Lead States, 2013; NRC, 2011) using the eight mathematical (Common Core State Standards Initiative, 2010) and science and engineering practices (NRC, 2011) to help explore and implement transdisciplinary curricula (i.e., multidisciplinary breadth) (figure 6.3).

The *Principles and Standards for School Mathematics* (National Council of Teachers of Mathematics [NCTM], 2000), *Benchmarks for Science Literacy* (American Association for the Advancement of Science [AAAS], 1993), and the *National Science Education Standards* [NSES] (NRC, 1996) advocate curricula emphasizing the integration of the STEM disciplines. Much of science is grounded in mathematics, and mathematics provides the machinery for making sense of the world in an analytical and quantitative fashion.

Science and engineering, on the other hand, provide a plethora of applications to which the theoretical underpinnings of mathematics can be applied. Too often, instruction underdevelops these important relationships. Strengthening the relationship among the STEM disciplines in both the educational and research venues will result in stronger, more cohesive learning and exploration in K–12 educational settings.

STEM PLUS allows preservice teachers the opportunity to experience the NGSS framework, the National Science Education Standards (NRC, 1996), and

Mathematical Practices	Crosscutting Concepts	Scientific and Engineering Practices
1. Make sense of problems and persevere in solving them	Patterns	1. Asking questions and defining problems.
2. Reason abstractly and quantitatively	Cause and Effect	2. Developing and using models.
3. Construct viable arguments and critique the reasoning of others	Scale, proportion and quantity	3. Planning and carrying out investigations.
4. Model with mathematics	Systems and systems models	4. Analyzing and interpreting data
5. Use appropriate tools strategically		5. Using mathematics and computational thinking
6. Attend to precision	Energy and matter	6. Constructing explanations and designing solutions
7. Look for and make use of structure	Structure and Function	7. Engaging in argument from evidence
8. Look for and express regularity and repeated reasoning	Stability and Change	8. Obtaining, evaluating, and communicating information

Figure 6.3 **Framework for transdisciplinary approach in STEM PLUS.** *Source*: author created.

the Common Core State Standards for Mathematics (CCSS-M) in a transdisciplinary manner within both formal and informal learning. Preservice teachers will formulate questions, engineer research methods, collect and analyze data, and communicate their findings in local and national contexts. Investigations will employ innovative technologies that will provide opportunities for future twenty-first–century educators to apply "outside of the box thinking to create solutions that will lead to results for students" (US DOE, 2010).

For example, previous research (Wilhelm, Sherrod, & Walters, 2008; Wilhelm, Jackson, Sullivan, & Wilhelm, 2012) on the effectiveness of the NASA-integrated REAL curriculum, a transdisciplinary curriculum, has shown that students and preservice teachers significantly improved their spatial-scientific thinking and understanding with significant transfer. Additional research has shown students making interdisciplinary connections and performing statistically significantly better on higher-order thinking assessments (Boaler, 2002; Polman, 2000).

Examples of Transdisciplinary STEM Curriculum and Instruction

STEM PLUS preservice teachers have experienced the Realistic Explorations in Astronomical Learning (REAL) curriculum (Wilhelm, Sherrod, & Walters,

2008) in the Designing Project-Enhanced Environments in STEM Education course. This experience has bolstered content knowledge and generated insight and appreciation toward the value of transdisciplinary curricula.

The overall objectives of the REAL curriculum are to provide learners with (1) hands-on experiences of space science research; (2) the ability to both quantitatively and qualitatively understand the phases of the Moon, the origins and evolution of specific features on the surfaces of planetary bodies within our solar system, and the geologic principle of superposition and relative/absolute age dating; (3) the opportunity to learn significant space science and mathematics content in a project-enhanced, national standards–based manner, and develop spatial reasoning skills that will transfer to other STEM areas; (4) the confidence and ability to communicate their own scientific and mathematical thinking and to understand others' thinking; and (5) measurable gain scores on conceptual forms of assessment in both mathematics and science.

The CCSS-M and the NGSS framework both include practices or crosscutting concepts (figure 6.3) that contain spatial mathematical domains. For example, CCSS-M mathematical practice eight describes how students should "look for and express regularity and repeated reasoning" *(looking for patterns)* and the NGSS crosscutting concepts include *patterns, systems and system models, structure and function,* and *stability and change.*

CCSS-M practices declare that students should "model with mathematics" and NGSS practices assert how students should have experiences "developing and using models"—in which such modeling applications could include geometric systems modeling (e.g., Earth/Moon/Sun system, orbital motions, etc.). REAL emphasizes these practices and crosscutting concepts that are fundamental to the development of spatial visualization and Earth/Space understanding.

In another course offered in STEM PLUS, preservice teachers have the opportunity to learn how to design a project-based learning environment and how to design, develop, and implement their own project-based units. The key features within a well-designed, project-based classroom include (1) driving research questions; (2) benchmark lessons to ensure content knowledge background and project progress; (3) milestones (opportunities to present project status to peers and teachers to gain feedback); and (4) sharing final investigative findings as well as future follow-up research.

STEM PLUS preservice teachers also experience a research-based content course that focuses on sustainability viewed from a systems-thinking perspective. One of the global challenges of the twenty-first century is sustainable development (United Nations Educational, Scientific, and Cultural Organization, 2005). In its broadest terms, sustainability impacts not only the environment, but also expands to include issues related to the economic and societal domains.

Often these problems are addressed in isolation within a single field; thus, this course prepares preservice teachers to work synergistically across disciplines while applying an integrated, systems-based thinking approach to problem solving to achieve sustainability. In this STEM content support course, students from the colleges of education, engineering, design, and business have a unique opportunity to develop projects about real-time issues as members of a collaborative team, offering a rich transdisciplinary experience to address a pivotal social issue, such as on-campus living.

The STEM PLUS program employs a transdisciplinary instructional approach to "to engage students in investigations that allow them to confront their misconceptions and develop a scientific understanding" (NRC, 2005, p. 423). There is a growing body of literature pointing toward the positive benefits of transdisciplinary instruction and curricular development for both preservice and in-service teachers in the STEM disciplines (Adumat, Little, Bouwma-Gearhart, & Bouwma-Gearhart, 2012; Anguita, Osuna, Martinez, & Dimitriadis, 2001; Wilhelm, Sherrod, & Walters, 2008). Transdisciplinary environments, such as those described here, will allow preservice teachers the opportunity to experience the CCSS-M (Common Core State Standards Initiative, 2010), the NGSS framework (NRC, 2011) and the forthcoming standards, and the National Educational Technology Standards (International Society for Technology in Education [ISTE], 2008) in a manner consistent with the transdisciplinary needs of future students and our future societal needs (Klein, 2008).

Instruction in the STEM PLUS program provides preservice teachers the opportunity to make decisions relative to appropriate project-based and other activities for secondary students. STEM PLUS also helps preservice teachers develop reflective practices concerning their instruction, including skills to evaluate their own STEM teaching methods with respect to their students' learning. Preservice teachers develop high, reasonable expectations for all students and skills to develop effective instruction for all students.

As preservice teachers advance through STEM PLUS, they will encounter numerous opportunities to create and implement ever-more sophisticated transdisciplinary curriculum and instruction. As specialists in fostering students' active construction of STEM discipline knowledge and processes through inquiry, preservice teachers will possess key training that is critically in need of dissemination in their future schools. STEM PLUS preservice teachers will build the knowledge and dispositions needed to engage as professional-development leaders in the schools in which they will serve.

A Clinical Approach to Teacher Education

In September 2011, the Education Profession Standards Board (EPSB) joined several other states across the United States in adopting the "10 Design Principles for Clinically Based Preparation" (National Council for the Accreditation of Teacher Education [NCATE], 2010), asking all teacher education programs throughout Kentucky to re-examine and "turn upside down" (p. ii) their programs. As a research-based, sound aspect for teacher preparation (NRC, 2010), clinically based preparation places a high focus on practice in the classroom. Throughout their undergraduate program, preservice teachers in the STEM PLUS program will have the opportunity to practice on a regular basis because they will take an education course each semester that contains a *course-embedded field experience*.

In a course-embedded field experience, preservice teachers are given release time from the course to ensure they have adequate time to complete their observation hours. During these placements, preservice teachers have focused activities and experiences that they must complete akin to the topic of their course.

Prior to student teaching, preservice teachers will have obtained at least 255 hours of hands-on experience with adolescents in classrooms and nontraditional settings, which is well above the Kentucky-required minimum of two hundred hours. In line with the NCATE's *Blue Ribbon Panel's Call to Action*, preservice teachers will spend their final year with one mentor teacher to practice in the same classroom, school, and community setting from the beginning of the school year to the end.

Field Experiences Embedded in Coursework

One of the eight STEM education courses will be taken each semester of the STEM PLUS program beginning as early as freshmen year. In each, there is a targeted clinical learning experience in a high-needs district (poverty >50 percent) before student teaching. During these placements, preservice teachers will have the opportunity to observe teaching and learning in diverse secondary-school settings, to coteach lessons with mentor teachers in the field, and to practice pedagogical techniques with their peers.

Table 6.2 displays the education coursework with the embedded field experience. For each of these experiences, candidates develop lesson plans, implement instruction, assess learning, reflect, and refine their own teaching and learning.

Table 6.2 Embedded Field Experiences

Course	Topics	Field Experience
Foundations of STEM Education (2 credit hours)	Addressing the following topics at an introductory level to give an overview of STEM Education: STEM education; education background; positive behavioral management; school law; learning theories; secondary schools; inquiry; environmental education; STEM literacy; differentiated instruction.	30 hours minimum in one classroom. The goal is to expose the student to the classroom from an observational perspective and make sure they really want to be a teacher. Reflections will center on general observations.
Education and American Culture (3 credit hours)	Critical examination of contending views, past and present, regarding the nature and role of educational institutions in US society as well as proposed purposes and policies for schools and other educational agencies.	30 hours minimum: 15 hours in formal setting and 15 hours in informal setting. The goal is to focus on the current nature of schools, the purpose of schools, and policy implications.
Human Development and Learning (3 credit hours)	Differentiated instruction; diversity; learning theories, specific strategies for motivating students (especially STEM); human psychological development, especially adolescents; adolescent learning.	20 hours minimum in formal and informal settings. Focus will be on exploring various theories of learning and adolescent development and motivations.
Special Education Strategies for STEM Education (3 credit hours)	Differentiated instruction, diversity, inclusive classrooms, 504, IEP, IDEA, TIP, ARC, collaborative classrooms, strategies for STEM classrooms, technology integration. The importance of being a part of a multidisciplinary team that develops an IEP will be stressed. Role-playing will be used extensively.	40 hours minimum in collaborative classroom(s). Focus will be on working with students with special needs in collaborative settings and learning basic tenets to differentiating instruction for these students. Will be required to attend IEP, 504, and ARC meetings.

(Continued)

Table 6.2 Continued

Course	Topics	Field Experience
STEM Methods I (3 credit hours)	Project-based instruction, forms of inquiry, modeling-based inquiry, differentiated instruction, diversity, curriculum knowledge (including state standards), positive behavioral interventions, unit and lesson planning, beginning development of philosophy of teaching STEM, classroom management, technology integration, creation of project-based unit.	100 hours minimum. Focus will be on implementing project-based instruction through modeling-based inquiry and hands-on experiences with general classroom structure and procedures. Students will have the opportunity to coteach lessons, teach mini-lessons, and work with individual and small groups of students.
STEM Methods II (3 credit hours)	Project-based instruction, modeling-based inquiry, implementation of project-based and MBI curriculum, classroom management, differentiated instruction, unit and lesson planning, further development of philosophy of teaching STEM, development of teacher portfolio, technology integration.	Beginning of year-long clinical student teaching placement. 100 hours required. Focus will be on implementation of knowledge for teaching the specific content, integration of STEM, and project-based instruction. Students will have several teaching and coteaching opportunities (will specifically teach developed project-based, MBI curriculum), and work with individual and groups of students.
Assessment in STEM Education (2 credit hours)	Differentiated instruction, diversity, general assessment knowledge, Unbridled Learning, developing effective tests, formative assessments, reading and interpreting assessment data, especially standardized assessments, using assessment data to inform instructional decisions, achievement gaps, data-driven decision making, making accommodations in assessment, equity issues in assessments especially related to high-stakes testing,	Part of the year-long clinical experience second half is student teaching. Will include assessment of candidate-developed project-based MBI curriculum.

(Continued)

Table 6.2 Continued

Course	Topics	Field Experience
Student Teaching (10 hours)	Gradually pick up classroom responsibilities. Minimum 20 days of full classroom responsibility and then gradually give classes back.	Continuation of year-long clinical student teaching experience. Minimum of 75 days in the classroom required.
TOTAL: 29 hours		>920 hours (320 hours prior to student teaching)

SAMPLE PRESERVICE TEACHER CANDIDATE TRAJECTORY

As highlighted, students in the STEM PLUS program have the opportunity to participate in a unique, groundbreaking program in which transdisciplinary and focused field experiences are central tenets. Table 6.3 shows the recommended course and field experience sequence for a STEM PLUS preservice physics teacher.

The dual major in the content area and in STEM Education is intentionally designed around the CCSS-M (Common Core State Standards Initiative 2010) and the framework for the NGSS, which includes engineering and engineering design standards. Throughout the program, preservice teachers experience, design, and implement STEM-integrated curricular units within both formal and informal learning environments in schools.

On successful completion of student teaching, a STEM PLUS preservice teacher is eligible to earn a Bachelor of Science with a double major in STEM Education and Mathematics, Physics, Chemistry, Computer Science, or Earth Science and, subsequently, certification for grades 8–12 for their content major area.

CONCLUSIONS AND IMPLICATIONS

STEM PLUS, an innovative and model transdisciplinary, clinically based secondary (grades 8–12) teacher program, seeks to dramatically increase the number of highly qualified, vastly effective mathematics and science teachers that have a transdisciplinary knowledge of STEM areas to increase student achievement in STEM disciplines and to encourage K–12 students to pursue STEM majors and careers. STEM PLUS is committed to producing STEM

Table 6.3 Sample Program Plan for STEM PLUS Physics Student

Year	Semester	Courses	Total Hours	Field Experiences
Freshman	Fall	• Calculus I; Communication Course; Gen. University Physics and Lab; Intro to Psychology	16	N/A
	Spring	• Calculus II; Intro to STEM Education; Optics, Relativity, and Thermal Physics; Gen. Chemistry I; Statistical Reasoning	16	30 hours in a middle- or high-school classroom
Sophomore	Fall	• Calculus III; Gen. University Physics II; Data Analysis for Physicists; Gen. Chem II; Human Development and Learning	17	30 hours in an informal-learning setting
	Spring	• Theoretical Models of Physics; Principles of Modern Physics; Citizenship Course; Communication Course; Education in American Culture	15	15 hours in an informal learning setting and 15 hours in a middle- or high-school classroom
Junior	Fall	• Topics in Astronomy and Astrophysics; Humanities Course; Special Education Methods Course; Systems Thinking for Sustainability; Digital Game-Based Learning	15	50 hours with a special-education collaborative teacher in a middle school or high school
	Spring	• Special Topics in Physics and Astronomy for Teachers; Humanities Course; STEM Methods I; Global Energy Issues; Intro. to Computer Programming	15	100 hours in a middle- or high-school classroom; 30 hours in an informal setting via the mathematics clinic at a middle school or high school
Senior	Fall	• STEM Methods II; Active Learning Lab for Secondary Physics Teachers; Personal Investing and Financial Planning; Photography I (free elective)	14	Begin year-long placement: 100 hours in a high-school classroom; Participation in the STEM Leadership Network
	Spring	• STEM Student Teaching in the Secondary Classroom; Assessment in STEM Education	12	Second half of year-long placement: minimum of 75 days in a high-school classroom; Participation in the STEM Leadership Network
TOTALS			120	**325 hours prior to student teaching; ~925 hours total**

teachers who will function as ethical professionals, lifelong learners, and leaders in their schools and communities.

STEM PLUS graduates will lead, largely by example, but also through more formal opportunities, such as the unique professional-development activities that the STEM PLUS partners create for both new and veteran teachers and administrators.

Armed with means to capitalize on cultural and linguistic diversity as a means for making STEM knowledge and skills relevant and useful for all students, STEM PLUS graduates will champion STEM educational equity, which may allow all students to use STEM productively in their daily lives to achieve personal goals, participate as active citizens, and develop the STEM skills necessary for access to modern opportunities in their global technological society.

Implications

STEM PLUS serves as a sustainable regional and national model for the STEM education community, specifically for STEM teacher preparation programs attempting to better meet the needs of preservice teachers. The STEM PLUS program is the first program to offer a major in STEM Education. Several programs, including the University of Arizona and UTEACH, have programs that fall under a STEM Education umbrella, but their graduates still receive a degree in their particular area of concentration and the programs do not necessarily focus on the integration of mathematics and science.

STEM PLUS addresses an additional pressing national need: the lack of STEM teachers. Studying a novel STEM teacher education program as a whole will result in significant contributions to our understanding of the various pathways in teacher education. To this end, STEM PLUS will provide important scientific research pertaining to the program's continued efforts and will provide critical comparisons with other programs, both traditional and alternative, in an attempt to train secondary teachers in the STEM disciplines.

Ultimately, as a result of STEM PLUS, each of our students will exit the program with competency in their knowledge and skills concerning their specific content-area of focus, general STEM knowledge and skills, and a well-grounded, research-based understanding of and ability to implement best teaching practices that foster student achievement among diverse future student populations. The graduates of STEM PLUS will be poised to become successful classroom teachers within their school districts because of their STEM knowledge for teaching, especially in relation to the integration of STEM disciplines.

NOTES

1. The Education Profession Standards Board (EPSB) issues certificates according to rank. Rank 4 is an emergency/temporary provisional certificate. Rank 3 is a certificate for an individual completing an undergraduate certification program. Rank 2 is a certificate for an individual who has completed a master's degree. Rank 1 is a certificate for an individual who has completed 30 hours beyond the master's degree. Teachers are paid according to their rank and years of experience.
2. The EPSB issues "provisional" certificates for *all* Kentucky teachers coming out of an initial-preparation program. This does not reflect any less quality in terms of No Child Left Behind (NCLB). Rather, it is a designation that they are to participate in the first-year induction program titled KTIP: Kentucky Teacher Internship Program, required in KRS 161.030 and established in 16 KAR 7:010 (EPSB, 2007). To be fully certified in the state of Kentucky ("professional certificate"), one must successfully complete the KTIP program.

REFERENCES

Adumat, S., Little, D., Bouwma-Gearhart, J., & Bouwma-Gearhart, A. (2012). Modeling-based curriculum for STEM undergraduate classrooms: Unifying mathematics and biology through jungle mathematics. Presented at the University of Kentucky Third Annual STEM Symposium. Lexington, KY, February 3.

American Association for Employment in Education (AAEE). (2007). *Educator supply and demand in the United States*. Evanston, IL: Author.

American Association for the Advancement of Science (AAAS). (1993). *Benchmarks for science literacy*. New York, NY: Oxford University Press.

Anguita, R., Osuna, C., Martinez, A., & Dimitriadis, Y. (2001). CECI: A computer-assisted co-educational and transdisciplinary experience. In J. Price, D. Willis, N. Davis, & J. Willis (Eds.), *Proceedings of SITE 2001—Society for information technology and teacher education international conference* (pp. 1532–1534). Norfolk, VA: Association for the Advancement of Computing in Education (AACE).

Boaler, J. (2000). Mathematics from another world: Traditional communities and the alienation of learners. *Journal of Mathematical Behavior, 18*(4), 379–397.

Carney, J. P, Chubin, D. E., & Malcom, S. M. (2008). Education and human resources in the FY 2009 budget: Supporting the STEM pathway. In *The American Association for the advancement of sciences report XXXIII research and development FY 2009*. Committee on Science, Engineering, and Public Policy. Washington, DC. Retrieved November 10, 2010, from http://www.aaas.org/spp/rd/09pch4.htm.

Common Core State Standards Initiative. (2010). Common Core State standards for mathematics. Retrieved November 27, 2018, from http://www.corestandards.org/wp-content/uploads/math_standards1.pdf.

Council of Chief State School Officers (2005). State indicators of science and mathematics education. Retrieved from archive.sheeo.org/SOAR2/source.asp?linkid=1217.

Darling-Hammond, L. (1999). *Supply, demand, and quality in mathematics and science teaching.* Briefing for the National Commission on Mathematics and Science Education for the Twenty-First Century. Washington DC, September 17.

Darling-Hammond, L. (2000). Teacher quality and student achievement: A review of state policy evidence. *Education Policy Analysis Archives, 8*(1). Retrieved from http://olam.ed.asu.edu/epaa/v8n1/.

Education Professional Standards Board (EPSB). (2007). *EPSB Meeting Agenda.* June 18. Louisville, KY. Retrieved from http://www.epsb.ky.gov.

Fetler, M. (1999, March). High school staff characteristics and mathematics test results. Education Policy Analysis Archives, 7(9). Retrieved from http://epaa.asu.edu/epaa/v7n9.html.

Florida, R. (2005). The *flight of the creative class: The new global competition for talent.* New York: Harper Collins Publishers.

Foster, E. (2010). *A new equation: How encore careers in math and science education equal more success for students.* Washington, DC: National Commission for Teaching America's Future. Retrieved November 29, 2018, from https://files.eric.ed.gov/fulltext/ed512647.pdf.

Hill, H. C., Schilling, S. C., & Ball, D. L. (2004). Developing measures of teachers' mathematics knowledge for teaching. *Elementary School Journal, 105,* 11–30.

International Society for Technology in Education (ISTE). (2008). National educational standards for teachers (NETS-T). Retrieved from https://people.umass.edu/pelliott/reflections/netst.html.

Hirsch Hardon, G., Hoffmann-Riem, H., Biber-Klemm, S., Grossenbacher-Mansuy, W., et al. Eds. (2008) *Handbook of transdisciplinary research.* New York: Springer Science + Business Media.

Klein, J. T. (2008). Education. In J. Jäger (Ed.), *Handbook of transdisciplinary research* (pp. 399–410). New York: Springer Science + Business Media.

Klein, J. T., Grossenbacher-Mansuy, W., & Häberli, R. (2001). *Transdisciplinarity: Joint problem solving among science, technology, and society: An effective way for managing complexity.* Boston, MA: Birkhauser.

Kuenzi, J. J. (2008). *CRS report for congress: Science, technology, engineering, and mathematics (STEM) education: Background, federal policy, and legislative action.* Updated March 21, 2008. Retrieved March 9, 2010, from www.fas.org/sgp/crs/misc/rl33434.pdf.

Monk, D. H. (1994). Subject area preparation of secondary mathematics and science teachers and student achievement. *Economics of Education Review,* 13, 125–145.

National Academy of Sciences. (2007). *Rising above the gathering storm: Energizing and employing america for a brighter economic future.* Washington, DC: National Academy Press.

National Commission on Excellence in Education. (1983). *A nation at risk: The imperative for educational reform.* Washington, DC: Government Printing Office.

National Council of Teachers of Mathematics (2000). *Principles and standards for school mathematics.* Reston, VA: NCTM.

National Council for the Accreditation of Teacher Education (NCATE). (2010). *Transforming teacher education through clinical practice: A national strategy to prepare effective teachers.* A Report of the Blue Ribbon Panel on Clinical Preparation and Partnerships for Improved Student Learning. Washington, DC: Author.

National Research Council (NRC). (1996). *National Science Education Standards.* Washington, DC: The National Academies Press. Retrieved from www.nap.edu/catalog.php?record_id=4962.

NRC (2001). *Educating teachers of science, mathematics, and technology: New practices for the millennium.* Washington, DC: National Academy Press.

NRC. (2005). *How students learn: History, mathematics, and science in the classroom.* Washington, DC: National Academies Press.

NRC. (2010). *Preparing teaches: Building evidence for sound policy.* Washington, DC: National Academies Press.

NRC. (2011). *A framework for K–12 science education: Practices, crosscutting concepts, and core Ideas.* Washington, DC: National Academies Press.

NGSS Lead States. (2013). *Next generation science standards: For states, by states.* Washington, DC: National Academies Press.

Nicolescu, B. 2002. *Manifesto of transdisciplinarity.* Albany, NY: SUNY Press.

Polman, J. L. (2000). *Designing project-based science: Connecting learners through guided inquiry.* New York, NY: Teachers College Press.

Romey, W. D. (1975). Transdisciplinary, problem-centered studies: Who is the integrator? *School Science and Mathematics, 75*(1), 30–38.

United Nations Educational, Scientific, and Cultural Organization. (2005). *United Nations decade of education for sustainable development (2005–2014): International implementation scheme.* Retrieved November 29, 2018, from http://unesdoc.unesco.org/images/0014/001486/148654e.pdf.

US Department of Education (US DOE). (2010). Transforming American education. Retrieved from https://www.ed.gov/sites/default/files/netp2010.pdf.

US Department of Labor, Employment and Training Administration. (2007). The STEM workforce challenge: The role of the public workforce system in a national solution for a competitive science, technology, engineering, and mathematics (STEM) workforce. Retrieved November 29, 2018, from www.doleta.gov/youth_services/pdf/stem_report_4%2007.pdf.

Wilhelm, J., Sherrod, S., & Walters, K. (2008). Experiencing project-based learning environments: Challenging pre-service teachers to act in the moment. *The Journal of Educational Research, 101*(4), 220–233.

Wilhelm, J., Jackson, C., Sullivan, A. & Wilhelm, R. (2012). Factors influencing middle school students' spatial mathematics development while participating in an integrated STEM unit. Proceedings of the Thirty-fourth Annual Meeting of the North American Chapter of the International Group for the Psychology of Mathematics Education. (PME-NA – Kalamazoo, MI).

Chapter 7

Troubling STEM

Making a Case for an Ethics and STEM Partnership

Astrid Steele

As part of my science-methods class, teacher–candidates (TCs) are introduced to integrated STEM activities through a tower-building competition. Essentially, groups of TCs are provided the scenario that they are stranded on an island after a plane crash.

The size of this imaginary island is such that its circumference can be hiked in two or three days, and it is inhabited by an indigenous population. To be rescued, the TCs must build a tower for the purpose of sending and receiving radio signals. After a cursory lesson on the impact of wind on tall structures, they are given limited supplies (e.g., one piece of cardstock, scissors, a meter of tape, and a 10-cm square of foil) for the purpose of constructing a tower.

It must be tall, it must withstand winds from the ocean, and it must support a properly shaped radio signal dish. The TCs set to work, using their knowledge of science and technology, coupled with attention to mathematical factors, to engineer a tower taller and stronger than those of their peers. The mood in the classroom is one of enthusiasm and excitement; the TCs like the competitive nature of the activity and the opportunity to problem solve in a team with simple materials. The theme of an old TV show, *Gilligan's Island*, plays in the background.

At first glance, the tower-building activity encapsulates science, technology, engineering, and math (STEM) at its finest: bright, young minds eagerly working to solve a specific and important problem that requires the integrated understanding and manipulation of STEM principles and skills. It seems hard to argue against a classroom activity that elicits so much eager, collaborative work applied to a problem requiring integrated STEM skills and knowledge. Surely, this is exactly what the creators of the Common Core State Standards

(CCSS) and the more recently released Next Generation Science Standards (NGSS; 2013) had in mind for students.

However, I have become increasingly troubled by the STEM initiative as it is playing out both in the United States and in Canada where I reside and work. Concerns are best addressed by examining the STEM initiative from three perspectives: the origins of STEM (because the circumstances precipitating the inception of an education initiative will inform its implementation); an examination of the type of knowledge that is created via STEM education (using as a framework Jürgen Habermas's threefold knowledge typology); and by way of a history lesson provided by Freeman Dyson, a noted US physicist. Taken together, the origins of STEM, a historical context, and an examination of knowledge theory, will bring into focus a troubling aspect of STEM—its apparent lack of a grounding in ethics.

I will use the tower-building activity as a backdrop for a discussion of the influence of the STEM initiative on education, taking into account the CCSS and the NGSS, and thereby clarify the need for STEM teaching and learning to realize the necessity of partnering with ethics education. An ethical framework for STEM would inform the decisions and directions of teachers and educators of teachers, as they navigate the sometimes-confusing pathways of integrated STEM curriculum.

ORIGINS OF STEM

In the 2009 Programme for International Student Assessment (PISA) study (Organisation for Economic Co-operation and Development [OECD], 2010), US students ranked seventeenth in international science and math assessments, well behind countries like Japan, China, and Korea and also behind Poland, Iceland, and Canada. The 2012 PISA study (OECD, 2013) again placed US students below the OECD international average scores in mathematics, science, and reading.

The poor performance of US students on the international stage continues to be a troubling state of affairs for the United States, a country that has viewed itself as a world leader politically, economically, and technologically for more than a century. It also explains the fierce drive to improve STEM education as a means to maintaining the nation's position as a global leader.

In 2004, seeing the writing on the wall, the US federal government invested $3 billion in STEM education programs through the National Science Foundation and the National Institutes of Health (Burke & Baker McNeill, 2011). In 2011, with the reauthorization of the America COMPETES Act, the focus on STEM education was renewed, and the industry responded with enthusiasm.

A coalition of corporate executive officers (CEOs) of some of the wealthiest and most influential companies in corporate America (e.g., Xerox and IBM) launched Change the Equation[1]—a philanthropic powerhouse that provides both money ($5 million in its first year) and programing to inspire STEM education. This is in keeping with the dual charge by the President's Council of Advisors on Science and Technology (PCAST; 2010) to inspire students and prepare them for careers in STEM.

But one should ask: What are students being prepared for? What are they being inspired for? In the report on STEM Education by the Heritage Foundation, Machi (2009) clearly and specifically identifies US industrial and defense capabilities as being seriously impaired by the decline in US students' interest in STEM education and STEM careers. In his January 2011 State of the Union Address, President Barack Obama said, "We need to out-innovate, out-educate, and out-build the rest of the world." Echoing the president's words, Change the Equation insists that "STEM is the future. STEM learning is an economic imperative."[2]

A 2011 Whitehouse government blog states: "The decisions we make today about how we invest in research and development, education, innovation, and competitiveness will profoundly influence our Nation's economic vitality, global stature, and national security tomorrow."[3] As it is reflected in both the political and industrial national discourses, the origin and intention of STEM education and knowledge generation in the United States is, undeniably, to buttress national economic and military capacity.

But STEM education is not a comprehensive form of knowledge, despite the interdisciplinarity implied in the acronym. In the same way that scholars have taken up the study of the nature of science to clarify its parameters and limitations, the "nature of STEM" also requires further definition and explication. For this task, I will look, in part, to the work of Jürgen Habermas.

HABERMAS'S KNOWLEDGE INTERESTS

Habermas proposed that all knowledge is bound up in the interests of the humans who generate and use it (Crotty, 2010). He categorized human knowledge using a threefold typology of "knowledge interests," the first of which is focused on the human need to survive and thrive. Certainly, the knowledge embedded in STEM disciplines does just that, enabling us to use natural resources and control environments to our benefit. Humans have created, as examples, complex habitation and transportation infrastructures and food-production systems based on our knowledge development in the STEM disciplines. Both the CCSS for Mathematics and the NGSS for science teaching and learning are clear examples of Habermas's first knowledge interest; they provide logical and sequential frameworks for content knowledge acquisition in classrooms.

Habermas's second knowledge interest encompasses humans' need to communicate knowledge among ourselves and come to some agreement around issues of language and social structure. This knowledge interest is partially supported in STEM education through the CCSS for Language Arts and Literacy in History/Social Studies, Science, and Technical Studies, which call for strengthened communication skills development. The STEM disciplines themselves have a well-developed, arguably hegemonic scientific symbology, and STEM disciplines currently hold a privileged place in the knowledge hierarchies of the western world (Gruenewald, 2004).

In his analysis of Habermas's work, Crotty (2010) posits that the first two knowledge interests function together to maintain the status quo. This certainly seems to be the intention of the STEM initiatives in the United States as evidenced by the stated desire to continue in a dominant international economic, political, and military position. However, Habermas's third knowledge interest should give STEM proponents some pause.

The third knowledge interest is of an emancipatory nature. It encourages critical self-reflection and addresses human responsibility regarding the use of the knowledge that is generated and communicated. The third knowledge interest enables choice making for what lies ahead. "It is precisely by imagining a future and taking steps to achieve the imagined future that humans can break out of the cultural system into which they have been socialized" (Crotty, 2010, p. 635). It is the third knowledge interest that underscores one of the weaknesses of the STEM initiative: as imagined by advocates of STEM, the future will be one of management and maintenance of the status quo for the United States as world leader.

In the service of a nation, the imagined future will continue to accede prestigious positions to STEM disciplines rather than encouraging a critique of that hegemony. Such an approach is neither emancipatory nor does it recognize a need for a critique of past political and economic strategies. Neither the CCSS nor the NGSS provide a strong platform for critical thinking within the STEM disciplines; rather they are both concerned with the acquisition and communication of knowledge.

Unfortunately, the generation of knowledge associated with the STEM disciplines has, in the past, been coopted for the purpose of lining the pockets of the already wealthy and resulted in collateral damage that includes laying waste to natural environments and further disenfranchising societies in the developing world. Most would agree that our future requires careful and thoughtful consideration, yet at this point, we might be most enlightened by looking to the past.

A LESSON FROM HISTORY

In the study of STEM pedagogies, it is often instructive to open the doors of interdisciplinarity and take a lesson from history. In his book *Disturbing the Universe* (1979) Freeman Dyson, a distinguished US physicist and author, acknowledges that science cannot be separated from the politics of human agency, which in so many cases, drives science forward. "We are scientists second and human beings first. We become politically involved because knowledge implies responsibility" (p. 6).

Dyson takes this idea further by suggesting that it is the obligation of the scientist (and we might add the STEM-literate teacher and citizen) to realize that STEM endeavors cannot be separated from a moral conscience. Reflecting on his time working as a technician in World War II British Bomber Command (which enabled the devastating destruction of cities like Dresden), Dyson recounts the burden of a moral conscience and the eventual collapse of his moral framework:

> I began to look backward and to ask myself how it happened that I let myself become involved in this crazy game of murder. . . . At the beginning of the war I fiercely believed in the brotherhood of man, called myself a follower of [Gandhi], and was morally opposed to all violence. After a year of war I retreated and said, Unfortunately nonviolent resistance against Hitler is impracticable, but I am still morally opposed to bombing. A few years later I said, Unfortunately it seems that bombing is necessary in order to win the war, and so I am willing to go to work for Bomber Command, but I am still morally opposed to bombing cities indiscriminately. After I arrived at Bomber Command I said, Unfortunately it turns out that we are after all bombing cities indiscriminately, but this is still morally justified as it is helping to win the war. A year later I said, Unfortunately it seems that our bombing is not really helping to win the war, but at least I am morally justified in working to save the lives of the bomber crews. In the last spring of the war I could no longer find any excuses. (p. 31)

Yet arguably, the most anguish-laden bombing of that war came in 1945 with the nuclear destruction of Hiroshima and Nagasaki. Dyson recollects the energy among the scientists at Los Alamos who designed and built those bombs: "While the work was going on, they were absorbed in scientific details and totally dedicated to the technical success of the project. They were far too busy with their work to worry about the consequences" (p. 52). The image of morally near-sighted scientists, funded by their government for military and political gain is troubling in itself, but it is certainly neither inconceivable nor surprising.

However, it is Dyson's further commentary that is particularly chilling: "But they did not just build the bomb. They enjoyed building it. They had the best time of their lives while building it" (p. 53). This image of scientists at work, happy to be entirely absorbed in their scientific endeavors, ceding their moral position to the government and military, should give all STEM educators pause. We need to continue to ask ourselves the questions: What are students being prepared for? What are they being inspired for?

History teaches that the STEM disciplines pursued with a narrow focus on knowledge creation become a seductive enterprise that can have unforeseen and horrific impacts on the lives of millions. With this history lesson in mind, we return to the classroom of TCs building towers to check on their progress.

A CHALLENGE FOR THE TOWER BUILDERS

As with many classroom construction projects, such as building the strongest bridge or creating the model airplane with the straightest, longest flight path, students are encouraged by the teacher to focus all of their knowledge, skill, and creativity on the task at hand. There is no hint that a stronger bridge or a better airplane should be anything but beneficial for its builders.

Halfway through the tower-building activity, another element to the competition is introduced. The TCs are reminded that they are on an inhabited island, and that, as they continue building, they must also consider and list the impacts that their stay will have on the island and on its indigenous population. By creating such a list, it is the intention to challenge the tower builders to consider the wide-reaching effects of their enterprise, that is, to introduce the idea that such an enterprise might require moral choices and an ethical position.

Some groups relegate the impact list task to the TC with the least inclination for engineering, whereas other groups begin an animated discussion as they work. The assignation of responsibility for the impact list mirrors STEM endeavors past and present: in some cases, as in the Los Alamos lab, impacts and ethics were left to the non-scientists. In my classroom, where nonscience majors far outnumber the science majors, there is genuine interest among many of the participants to deliberate over the consequences of their imaginary stay on the island.

The resulting lists of predicted impacts are telling. They reveal prevalent and deeply ingrained attitudes about the competitive, unsustainable, and colonizing legacy of a historical version of STEM. Most groups identify that their stay may strain the food and natural-resources supply on the island, certainly create waste, and possibly introduce new pathogens. Some groups will suggest that the native populations will benefit by being exposed to new technologies and learning about new medicines.

There is an overarching assumption that the tower builders can go about their task and actually build the tower without negotiation or acknowledgement that they are inhabiting the space previously occupied by others. The TCs work within a paradigm in which they have an implicit right to cut the trees, build their shelters, and harvest the food on the island. For the most part, their imagined interactions with the inhabitants are treated as necessities to furthering their own interests.

Of course, there are exceptions, and these can also be revealing. One group of young women completely gave up on building a tower and decided that they would survive by marrying into the native population. They had no interest in the STEM initiative of tower building and felt that, given their social abilities and feminine wiles, they could live out their lives happily on the island as wives and mothers.

In another session, during a discussion of relationships between the islanders and the castaways, a young First Nations woman in my class asked her peers why they thought the indigenous people on the island would need or want new technologies or medicines. Her hinted reference to her people's colonized past became a powerful moment for the class as they made the connection between their imaginary activity and her historic reality.

THE TROUBLE WITH STEM

Although both economic and military capacities are justifiable national priorities, it is instructive to attend to what remains unsaid. US STEM rhetoric does not focus on making a better world, or a sustainable world, or improving the lives of oppressed around the world. The discourse focused on STEM initiatives neither explicitly nor implicitly addresses pressing global issues. Perhaps there are reasons that STEM seems distasteful to students, beyond teachers who have been targeted as unprepared to teach those subjects. The young people with whom I have worked have often been drawn to causes bigger than themselves, to building a better world, and taking seriously their responsibilities as global citizens.

Despite its claims of interdisciplinarity, STEM exerts a single-minded focus on science, technology, engineering, and math as the means to strengthening US interests nationally and globally. The intention that STEM education will improve the lives of people, or environments, both locally and globally, is largely ignored, unless it is in the best interests of US generation of wealth and national defense. Fortunately, there is a growing awareness that the STEM drive must be tempered by a balancing drive from the humanities and social sciences (Johnson, 2010). Single-mindedness will not serve a human future as well as a holistic approach informed by many and varied voices.

To that end has come a call for socio-scientific studies within STEM curricula; these examine STEM issues in social and environmental contexts and have as their goal "education for citizenship" (Levinson, 2006). Studies that examine the impacts of science and technology on society and environment (STSE), embedded in science teaching and learning, have become common in many curricula in, for example, Canada, the United Kingdom, and Australia (Driver, Newton, & Osborne, 2000; Kolstø, 2001).

Of particular interest to this chapter is that STSE studies tend to bring into focus the moral position of an individual or the society in which they live. When called on to critically analyze social and environmental issues and cases that result from STEM activities (e.g., embryo design or genetically modified foods), students often find themselves faced with making moral choices (De Luca, 2010; Herreid, Schiller, & Herreid, 2012; Reiss, 2010).

In a workbook called *Science Stories: Using Case Studies to Teach Critical Thinking* (Herreid et al., 2012), there is an entire section, comprising eight cases, devoted to applying ethics and the scientific method to individual cases. The cases are based on actual events and come with prepared questions for students and notes for the teacher. The careful preparation and presentation of such a workbook for teachers in the STEM disciplines is laudable because it provides them with the tools (e.g., cases, guiding questions, extra notes) for classroom implementation.

However, not present in the workbook is mention of the study of ethics as a discipline, with a methodology that includes various lines of reasoning and a system of frameworks that might be applied in various situations. One could argue that without explicit ethics education, including possible ethical frameworks to guide moral choices, neither teachers nor their students are fully prepared to engage in the task of case analysis. Ethics instruction is not addressed in the CCSS or the NGSS, neither does it hold much prominence in teacher preparation or professional development; ethics education continues to be elusive in classrooms. Nonetheless, it is not entirely absent; there are doubtless many morally motivated, thoughtful educators who understand the need to introduce their students to issues that require critical and ethical thinking.

The argument here is that ethics education should not remain implicit in curriculum, addressed occasionally by a handful of teachers; rather, ethics education should be incorporated with cogency in curricular documents. Ethics education should take its place in a partnership with STEM studies; it is critical to provide our students and their teachers with the tools to critique STEM activities and directions and to make wise choices as global citizens. The question then becomes: What might ethics education for a STEM partnership look like?

ETHICS FOR STEM

Herreid et al. (2012) describe ethics simplistically as dealing with "questions of good and evil, right and wrong, virtue and vice, and justice and injustice" (p. 268). The dualism implied by those words suggests a line of thinking that does not do justice to the complexity of most ethical dilemmas and may thereby compromise the process of critical analysis. In my experience, the young people who engage in classrooms are often passionate about their choices, but at the same time, they are still developing their ethical reasoning abilities (Reiss, 2010). To present either–or choices regarding ethical dilemmas does not support students' progress in learning to make complex reasoned decisions.

Ethics is defined by Reiss (2010) as "a branch of philosophy concerned with how we should decide what is morally wrong and what is morally right" (p. 7). Although apparently dualistic in nature, Reiss's definition focuses on the decision-making process and links the concept of morality to a critical analysis of actions in particular circumstances. Critical analysis can take a number of different paths of reasoning; indeed, there is more than one ethical framework that would inform and support STEM studies.

However, the intention of this chapter is not to present a comprehensive inventory of ethical frameworks, but rather to put forward the benefits of partnering STEM with ethics education in teacher education. Along with content and skill-rich STEM learning, De Luca (2010) asserts that teachers can provide their students with "robust ethical frameworks for understanding and appraising applications and implications" (p. 87). The next section examines three ethical frameworks particularly suitable for the integrated STEM classroom and applies these to the work of the tower builders.

Consequentialism

Reasoning through an ethical dilemma using a framework based on consequentialism requires an interrogation of possible outcomes of the decisions being made. Questions might include:

- Who or what is affected by this issue?
- What are the benefits involved?
- What are the harms for those involved?
- Are some consequences greater or lesser than others?
- If one is harmed and another benefits, how do you decide who or what matters most? (McKim, 2010, p. 31)

Additional questions might be:

- Can we know all of the consequences of actions with respect to the issue of focus?
- Is there a legitimate time frame within which to consider the consequences of our actions?
- What should you do to be sure your actions are based on a full consideration of the consequences? (Steele, Brew, & Beatty, 2012)

The secondary assignment to the tower builders in my classroom, to determine the impacts of their presence on the island, is rooted in the consequentialism framework. Based on their combined prior personal knowledge gained as a result of their undergraduate studies, the TCs have to brainstorm the environmental and social consequences of their living and working on the imaginary island. One of the benefits of using the consequentialism framework is the resultant consolidation of STEM content knowledge and skills.

Consequentialism, partnered with a STEM topic in an elementary or secondary classroom, offers students starting points for further investigations that will allow them to reason from well-informed positions. For example, in deciding on the acceptance of genetically modified foods, questions such as: What are the benefits involved and what are the harms for those involved? Provide students with further directions for investigations into the specific technologies used in genetic manipulation.

Virtues Ethics

Virtues-ethics support and build on character education, which is itself a recent initiative in education. Within a virtues-ethics framework, reasoning is based on what characteristics constitute a morally "good" or virtuous individual. For example, it is morally correct for a teacher to be fair to all students, rather than favoring all of the girls or all of the Toronto Maple Leafs supporters (Reiss, 2010). Questions that might be asked within the virtues-ethics framework are:

- How would you define a person of good character?
- What would a person of good character do in this situation?
- What characteristics or qualities would we want a person to manifest in this situation?
- How might a person of good character make questionable ethical decisions in this situation?

- Who decides what are the ideal qualities of a person with good character in this situation?
- What would you do in this situation? (Steele et al., 2012)

We would generally agree that most people see themselves as "good" people and would want others to see them that way as well. For the tower builders, the virtues ethics framework informs their decision making by urging them to consider the actions of a morally good person in their situation.

For example, if one of the islanders were to have an illness or injury that could be healed by the tower builders, a morally good person would provide that healing. But given the loss of traditional healing and medicine expertise in the face of advancing Western medicine, one might additionally ask: Would a morally good person expose the islanders to Western medicine at all? Would a morally good person value and respect indigenous medicine to the point of agreeing to withhold Western medicine?

Sustainability Ethics

With an increasing interest and need to consider the limitations of the planet's resources and the Brundtland Commission's (1987) directive that those living now shoulder a socioenvironmental responsibility for future generations, it is not surprising to find a branch of ethics tackling issues of sustainability. According to Kibert, Monroe, Peterson, Plate, and Thiele (2012), a sustainability ethic addresses the future by juxtaposing the needs and rights of the present with the needs and rights of the future.

Questions that might frame sustainability ethics are:

- Can future individuals have rights?
- How is it possible to address the needs of future peoples when the needs of the vast majority of the world's present population are not being met?
- What exactly are the "needs" that must be met and how might these be prioritized? (Kibert et al., 2012, p. 15)

We can also ask:

- Should we only consider the future rights and needs of humans? What about animals? Plants?
- Does the "environment" have rights?

Sustainability ethics might also find purchase in Habermas's third knowledge interest regarding the choices we make for the future. By asking some of the questions posed, we bring clarity to the significance of our STEM knowledge and further understand the responsibility such knowledge imparts for future choices. The TCs' tower-building exercise does not grapple with sustainability ethics until the challenge of the impact list is introduced.

At that point, the TCs have to consider a picture broader in scope, not just for their present circumstances, but also for possible futures. Admittedly, the premise of the activity is that they should be rescued and leave the island rather quickly—a scenario that downplays the need for sustainable choices. However, the lasting impacts of their activities might reach far into an imaginary future for the island inhabitants and its environment. The TCs are asked to consider consequences that might play out long after they have departed.

THE TIME FOR ETHICS EDUCATION

At what point in their science and math studies should students be introduced to ethics education? This is a fair question and has been tackled by a number of developmental theorists, with exceptional research done by Lawrence Kohlberg (Crain, 1985). Kohlberg identified a number of stages in the moral development of individuals, beginning with a simple, externalized view of right and wrong and moving toward an internalized system of principles for a "good" society.

Of interest to educators is Kohlberg's contention that progress through the six stages of moral development is not related to maturation or socialization. Rather, students need to actually engage in the "cognitive conflict" that proceeds from grappling with an issue, which further encourages them to progressively develop their ideas of morality and ethics.

> As children interact with others, they learn how viewpoints differ and how to coordinate them in cooperative activities. As they discuss their problems and work out their differences, they develop their conceptions of what is fair and just. (Crain, 1985, p. 126)

In addition to Kohlberg's stages, Reiss (2010) suggests that as students move through degrees of moral development, they also are able to (1) use more than one ethical framework; (2) determine which is most useful in a given situation; (3) include forms of life other than humans in their deliberations; (4) consider long-term outcomes; and (5) integrate scientific knowledge and ethical principles. In a study of ethics education aimed at young students ages five to ten, Buntting and Ryan (2010) found that even young children can reason and justify their choices as long as the ethical issue being studied is familiar to the student.

It is thus appropriate to introduce ethics education at an early age in schooling, realizing that students must be supported as they examine complex issues and with the understanding that a moral conscience needs to be developed because it is not innate. The ability to reason morally within an ethical framework at a sophisticated level is a skill that requires nurturing and refining throughout one's life. The assumption that all adults, indeed, that all teachers, fully and consistently understand and act on their personal system of principles is ill-informed. This has significant implications for teacher training, as suggested by Buntting and Ryan (2010):

> Successful implementation (of ethics education) seems to centre on teacher knowledge in both the planning and implementation of authentic classroom experiences. As such the teacher needs to be able to integrate knowledge of the issue or topic with knowledge of ethical reasoning approaches. (p. 52)

Buntting and Ryan recommend professional-development workshops to train teachers in integrating ethics education within existing curriculum and, further, advocate for ongoing support for those educators. However, given that most teacher candidates have not had explicit ethics education, it would seem expedient to introduce ethics during initial teacher preparation and to partner it with STEM education during that training period.

ENGAGING STUDENTS AND TEACHERS

Perhaps one of the strongest arguments to be made for partnering STEM with ethics education is that such an approach will intrigue and engage students (Herreid et al., 2012). As discussed previously, STEM topics can often be coupled with socio-scientific, or STSE issues. Research suggests that an STSE perspective on STEM provides a pedagogical avenue that has been shown to increase student enjoyment and motivation for their science studies (Herreid, 2012; McKim, 2010).

> There is a price to pay for our typical approach in science, technology, engineering and math education, and for our devotion to facts, the lecture method and multiple choice tests. . . . Science majors have a high tolerance for boring material that seems to have nothing to do with their lives—a kaleidoscope of facts without apparent rhyme or reason. . . . (Nonscientists) are not intrigued by the detailed structure of the atom or the cell. It is not that they do not think it is important; they simply do not see why it should be important to them. We have not shown them how the cavalcade of facts relates to global warming, the debate over creationism versus evolution, natural disasters, cancer, AIDS, sex, or anything else they might care about. (Herreid, 2012, p. x)

Given the concern of the US government that high numbers of students seem to be opting out of STEM courses and programs, the premise that disciplines such as science and math, coupled with STSE and informed by ethics education will keep students enrolled and engaged in STEM programs should be enthusiastically explored. Moreover, when students can tackle their studies in formats that more fully integrate learning within STEM disciplines, STSE perspectives and critical thinking informed by ethics education, their learning is authentic and contextual.

One last visit to the tower builders in my classroom provides substantive evidence that the partnering of integrated STEM learning with STSE and ethics education has potential for student and teacher engagement. The TCs comment on how much fun they had building the towers but add that deliberating over the list of their impacts on the island added a necessary and important component to their task.

As they learn to become educators, the TCs increasingly see their own learning through a teacher's eyes. They recognize and value opportunities for integration, particularly when those opportunities incorporate critical thinking and ethical decision making.

CONCLUSION

In summary then, the STEM education initiative has its origins in the US desire to boost student interest and participation in science and math as a means to maintaining economic prosperity and strengthening national defense. Concurrently, the CCSS and the NGSS have added curricular structure to programs for language, mathematics, and science education.

However, inasmuch as the STEM initiative and the state standards for education address human knowledge interests in the past and present, Habermas's third knowledge interest points out the inherent weakness of the current approach, which is the lack of an explicitly stated, thoughtfully considered, and ethically reasoned global emancipatory future, and history provides examples of how easily the shortsighted and insular pursuit of STEM disciplines can yield destructive instruments that, in turn, bring forth unintended consequences and moral conflict. STEM educators should continue to ask the questions: What are students being prepared for? What are they being inspired for?

The tower-building activity intimates that STEM education has global repercussions that require the development of global sensibility and responsibility by both students and their teachers. STEM studies must be balanced; STEM education needs to be informed by the humanities and, most importantly, by ethics; this should be explicitly reflected in the CCSS and the NGSS.

A partnership between STEM and ethics education, through direct teaching of ethical frameworks, such as virtues ethics, consequentialism, and sustainability ethics, is strongly advocated for teacher training and development. Ethics education can be introduced to students at an early age and should support student moral development and ethical decision making throughout the years of schooling. It follows that teacher development in this respect is essential and should be part of teacher training.

Pursuing a partnership between STEM and ethics is worthwhile for many reasons, of which the most obvious is that students clearly are intrigued and motivated by the opportunity to grapple with difficult socio-scientific issues that require interdisciplinary critical thinking and moral reasoning. This addresses the immediate concerns that precipitated the STEM initiative: US students do not seem to be interested in pursuing STEM courses or careers.

However, clearly teacher education and ongoing professional development are necessities for the STEM and ethics partnership, as is the need to root these thoughtfully and masterfully in state standards for education. Because, most importantly, a STEM and ethics partnership will support the development of teachers who are STEM literate and morally mature—teachers who are able to support their students in taking global and national perspectives on STEM-related issues, thus enabling them to become capable and informed ethical decision makers.

NOTES

1. See http://changetheequation.org/.
2. See http://changetheequation.org/why-stem/.
3. See https://obamawhitehouse.archives.gov/blog/2011/01/06/america-competes-act-keeps-americas-leadership-target.

REFERENCES

Brundtland Commission (formally known as the World Commission on Environment and Development). (1987). *Our common future, report of the world commission on environment and development.* London, UK: Oxford University Press.

Bunting C., & Ryan, B. (2010). In the classroom: Exploring ethical issues with young pupils. In A. Jones, A. Mckim and M. Reiss, (Eds.), *ethics in the science and technology classroom: A new approach to teaching and learning* (pp. 37–54). Rotterdam, The Netherlands: Sense Publishers.

Burke, L. M., & Baker Mcneill, J. (2011). 'Educate to innovate.' How the obama plan for STEM education falls short. *Backgrounder, 25*(4), 1–8.

Crain, W. C. (1985). *Theories of development: Concepts and applications*. London, UK: Prentice-Hall.

Crotty, R. (2010). Values education as an ethical dilemma about sociability. In T. Lovat, R. Toomey, & N. Clement (Eds.), *International research handbook on values education and student well-being* (pp. 631–644). New York: Springer Science + Business Media.

Deluca, R. (2010). Using narrative for ethical thinking. In A. Jones, A. Mckim, & M. Reiss, (Eds.), *Ethics in the science and technology classroom: A new approach to teaching and learning* (pp. 87–102). Rotterdam, The Netherlands: Sense Publishers.

Driver, R., Newton, P., & Osborne, J. (2000). Establishing the norms of scientific argumentation in classrooms. *Science Education, 84*(3), 287–312.

Dyson, F. (1979). *Disturbing the Universe*. New York, NY: Harper & Row.

Gruenewald, D. A. (2004). A Foucauldian analysis of environmental education: Toward the socioecological challenge of the earth charter. *Curriculum Inquiry, 34*(1), 71–104.

Herreid, C. F. (2012). Introduction. In C. F. Herreid, N. A. Schiller, & K. F. Herreid (Eds.), *Science stories: Using case studies to teach critical thinking* (pp. vii–xiii). Arlington, VA: National Science Teachers Association Press.

Herreid, C. F., Schiller, N. A., & Herreid, F. K. (Eds.). (2012). *Science stories: Using case studies to teach critical thinking*. Arlington, VA: National Science Teachers Association Press.

Johnson, R. R. (2010). Balancing acts: A case for confronting the tyranny of STEM. *Programmatic Perspectives, 2*(1), 86–92.

Kibert, C. J., Monroe, M. C., Peterson, A. L., Plate, R. R., & Thiele, L. P. (2012). *Working toward sustainability: Ethical decision making in a technological world*. Hoboken, NJ: Wiley.

Kolstø, S. D. (2001). 'To trust or not to trust, . . .'—pupils' ways of judging information encountered in a socio-scientific issue. *International Journal of Science Education, 23*(9), 877–901.

Levinson, R. (2006). Teachers' perceptions of the role of evidence in teaching controversial socio-scientific issues. *The Curriculum Journal, 17*(3), 247–262.

Machi, E. (2009). *Improving US competitiveness: With K–12 STEM education and training*. Washington, DC: The Heritage Foundation.

Mckim, A. (2010). Bioethics education. In A. Jones, A. Mckim, & M. Reiss, (Eds.), *Ethics in the science and technology classroom: A new approach to teaching and learning* (pp. 1–5). Rotterdam, The Netherlands: Sense Publishers.

NGSS Lead States. (2013). *Next generation science standards: For states, by states*. Washington, DC: National Academies Press.

Organisation for Economic Co-operation and Development (OECD). (2010). PISA 2009 results: Executive summary. Retrieved November 29, 2018, from https://www.oecd.org/pisa/pisaproducts/46619703.pdf.

Organisation for Economic Co-operation and Development (OECD). (2013). PISA 2012 results in focus. Retrieved November 29, 2018, from http://www.oecd.org/pisa/keyfindings/pisa-2012-results-overview.pdf.

President's Council of Advisors on Science and Technology (PCAST). (2010). Prepare and inspire: K–12 education in science, technology, engineering, and math (STEM) for America's future. Report to the President. Retrieved November 29, 2018, from https://obamawhitehouse.archives.gov/sites/default/files/microsites/ostp/pcast-stem-ed-final.pdf.

Reiss, M. (2010). Ethical Thinking. In A. Jones, A. Mckim, & M. Reiss, (Eds.), *Ethics in the science and technology classroom: A new approach to teaching and learning* (pp. 7–18). Rotterdam, The Netherlands: Sense Publishers.

Steele, A., Brew C. R., & Beatty, B. R. (2012). The tower builders: A consideration of STEM, stse and ethics in science education. *Australian Journal of Teacher Education, 37*(10), 118–133.

Chapter 8

Preparing Science Teaching Candidates to Deliver Language-Rich STEM Instruction[1]

Kevin Carr and Jonathan Pope

How should twenty-first–century science teaching candidates be prepared for work in schools and communities that have student populations with high levels of poverty or English-language learners (ELLs)? One distinguishing feature of many such communities is the need to focus explicitly on the development of academic language literacy, bridging the gap between the everyday language of students and the academic language needed for success in college and careers. The Next Generation Science Standards (NGSS) emphasize demonstrating proficiency through communicating evidence-based arguments and reasoning, effectively embedding academic language skills within science content (or vice versa).

One challenge faced by both new and veteran science teachers implementing NGSS is seamlessly implementing rich academic language instruction within a content-driven curriculum. We illustrate how science teacher–candidates, mentor teachers, and science educators developed and used content-driven curriculum planning tools to create and implement literacy-rich science instruction (iSTEM). It is argued that supporting new science teachers to collaboratively implement iSTEM prepares them to seamlessly integrate academic literacy instruction into the science, technology, engineering, and math (STEM) curriculum, successfully preparing students in high-needs settings for STEM-literate careers and citizenship.

STEM LITERACY AND ACADEMIC LANGUAGE

How many talented young people are we losing in today's schools, driven by test scores that reward teachers for drilling students to remember obscure science words? Instead we should be rewarding them for teaching science inquiry skills and literacy together, through collaborative and critical discourse. (Alberts, 2010, p. 405)

The future of our communities, nation, and world depends on our ability to find innovative solutions to complex, technical, and often, sociopolitical, problems. The ongoing "STEM crisis" is often framed in terms of lagging international science and mathematics test score rankings (Organisation for Economic Co-operation and Development [OECD], 2012), concerns with the ability of the United States to compete in an increasingly STEM-based demanding global marketplace (President's Council of Advisors on Science and Technology [PCAST], 2010), and the continued STEM opportunity gap between middle-class students and their poorer, minority peers (Darling-Hammond, 2010). There is universal agreement on the urgent need for a different kind of STEM education, especially in high-poverty Latino communities in which many students are ill prepared for STEM careers (Rodriguez, 2012).

Specifically, a central science literacy skill is the ability to construct and communicate evidence-based arguments and reasoning; skill in communication is essential to not only STEM careers, but also to twenty-first–century citizenship. Evidence-based argumentation and reasoning enfolds the elements of science, math, and language literacy explicitly expressed in the Next Generation Science Standards (National Research Council [NRC], 2011), Common Core State Standards in Mathematics (Common Core State Standards Initiative, 2015), and English Language Proficiency Standards (ELPA21, 2014). We view science as a story that is told in the language of data, demonstrating how science and society interact with data, and detailing the evolution of ideas based on that interaction.

Success in school is contingent on the ability cope with, and become fluent in, academic language (Cummins, 2001; Gee, 2004). Still, many middle- and secondary-school science teachers resist the explicit teaching of communication skills, often arguing (understandably, in our view) that their role is to teach science, not English (McCoss-Yergian & Krepps, 2010). The teachers we work with perceive that professional development in teaching academic language literacy consists of training in (1) selecting "language goals" for each lesson and unit, and (2) designing separate "language activities" to add to their regular content instruction.

Our teachers often describe teaching science-language literacy as a separate and distinct task from teaching "science content," representing a loss in classroom instructional time (figure 8.1). Given the zero-sum nature of the way many teachers view teaching language literacy in science classes, it

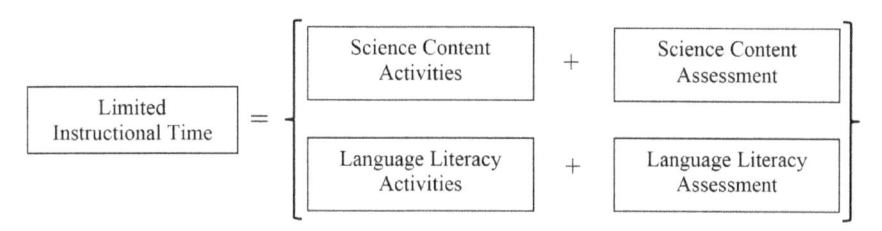

Limited Instructional Time = [Science Content Activities + Science Content Assessment / Language Literacy Activities + Language Literacy Assessment]

Figure 8.1 Zero-sum model of language and content instruction. *Source*: author created.

is not surprising that teachers struggle to develop language literacy in their students, often defaulting to content instruction with only cursory (at most) attention to language development. In fact, despite significant professional development, training, and coaching in language literacy, many of our partner science teachers report an urgent need for useful resources, models, and tools for language instruction (Kim, Carr, & Pope, 2014).

In contrast, research at the intersection of STEM education and language literacy suggests that science content and language learning are most likely driven by one another and that ELLs benefit from explicit instruction in the specialized vocabulary and language forms of science embedded in science content (Anders, 2012; Webb, 2010; Snow, 2010; Gee, 2008). Science literacy involves a dimension of synthesis, where multiple sources of data, opinion, speculation, and prediction must be aggregated together and critically evaluated so that a consistent scientific narrative results.

Evidence-based argumentation is particularly challenging for ELLs because this type of argumentation entails proficiency in "evidence-based arguments"; that is, the ability to interpret and analyze scientific data and discuss the data with proper evidence. Linguistically, this type of argumentation requires students to use complex linguistic structures; ELLs particularly have difficulty with making clear and coherent evidence-based arguments because of their limited language proficiency. We are developing a curriculum model that enfolds *multiple literacies*, including academic language, to reach the central goal of evidence-driven argumentation (figure 8.2).

For example, in the science classroom discourse shown, middle-school ELL students are prompted to construct a written or verbal response that embeds multiple literacies together within the understanding of science content. Students require a significant degree of language scaffolding to create and communicate an evidence-based argument at a high proficiency level (textbox 8.1).

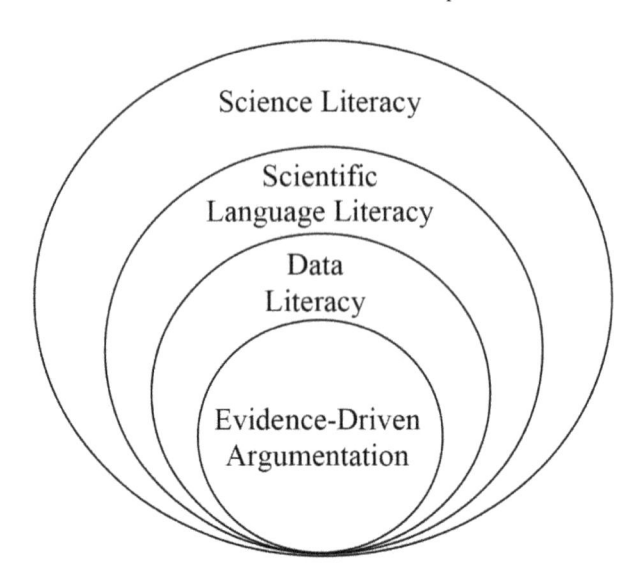

Figure 8.2 Multiple enfolded literacies in the science classroom. *Source*: author created.

TEXTBOX 8.1   TYPICAL SCIENCE CLASSROOM DISCOURSE

NGSS-Expected Proficiencies:

- *Develop a model that predicts and describes changes in particle motion, temperature, and state of a pure substance when thermal energy is added or removed.* (MS-PS1-4)
- *Collect data to provide evidence for how the motions and complex interactions of air masses results in changes in weather conditions.* (MS-ESS2-5)

Teacher: What do you think will happen when a warm, moist, unstable air mass meets a cold, stable, dry air mass? How do you know this? Explain.
Student: I predict _____. (low-level proficiency)
I predict that _____ *will* _____. (mid-level proficiency)
I predict that_____ *will* _____ *because* _____. (high-level or grade-level proficiency)

Proficient Student Response:	I predict that clouds and precipitation will occur because historical Oregon weather maps and data show the pattern that rain and snow was more likely to happen in areas where warm, ocean air had moved inland and mixed with colder, drier air. This is consistent with the kinetic model that predicts that when faster-moving warm water vapor molecules slow, they tend to adhere to one another, condensing into liquid water droplets, which form clouds and possibly precipitation.
Typical Student Response:	I predict that clouds and precipitation will occur because when warm, moist air cools, the water molecules slow and condense into clouds. An example of this is when a warm storm comes in from the coast and meets cold air in the valley and produces rain and snow.

At the conclusion of a unit on matter and its interactions, the teacher prompts the student to make a claim about the mixing of different air masses and to support the claim with evidence and reasoning. The proficient student response reveals the complex interfolding of model-based reasoning (kinetic model), data literacy (weather data), and complex vocabulary and language forms (cause-and-effect prediction, supported with evidence and explanation, using specialized academic vocabulary and register).

Our research, involving secondary-science teachers with a high degree of skill infusing language instruction in their curricula, shows that although ELL students often become proficient at communicating claims and model-based reasoning, they struggle to properly support their claims and reasoning and evidence. We believe that this is as a result of a lack of explicit attention to developing data- and language-literacy skills together in science instruction.

iSTEM: STRUCTURING LITERACY-RICH STEM UNITS

We use the term *iSTEM* to represent an integrated strategy in which literacy-rich lessons, units, and curricula can be reframed using a multiple-literacies approach. The goal is to help teachers think of and plan for language literacy not as a separate curricular objective, but instead in service of understanding the science content (figure 8.3).

iSTEM Curriculum Framework Tool

| Science Content Objective With Expected Student Academic Language | → | Literacy-Rich Science Content Activities | → | Content Assessment using Evidence-Based Argumentation |

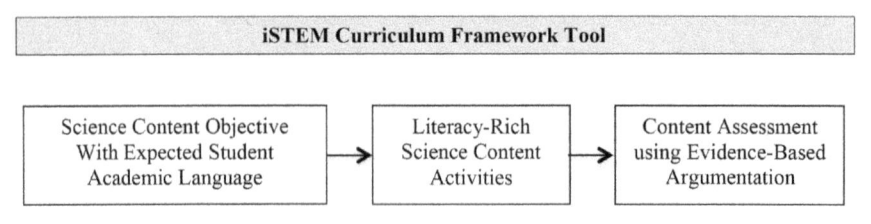

Figure 8.3 iSTEM model relating language and content instruction. *Source*: author created.

We have also designed tools to help teachers overcome their resistance to teaching data-language literacy as they plan lessons and curriculum. For example, we used the iSTEM Literacy Planning Tool (Curriculum Framework Tool [CFT]; figure 8.4) to help teachers plan instruction around the classroom discourse referenced in textbox 8.1.

The CFT guides the teacher to (i) select a content-based phenomenon or process with which students will work, (ii) create a written or verbal assessment prompt to evaluate student ability to perform the NGSS task within the given content context, and (iii) write a sample or "target" response to the prompt using expected academic vocabulary and language forms and functions. The teacher then examines the target response and generates a list of language stems and vocabulary designed to scaffold students to practice using academic language when they write and speak.

These language stems and vocabulary will be integrated into the lesson and materials to explicitly feature the needed academic language and to scaffold the work of students. Finally, the teacher may refer to materials and note which language forms and functions are featured in the model response, and if desired, may write one or more related language objectives, such as "I will learn to write and speak correct 'cause-and-effect' sentences."

ON TARGET:
iSTEM in a Fifth-Grade Bilingual Classroom

On Target is an engineering design challenge based on NASA's 2010 LCROSS (Lunar Crater Observation and Sensing Satellite) mission (WGBH Educational Foundation, https://www.nasa.gov/pdf/418005main_OTM_On_Target.pdf). LCROSS was designed to detect water ice on the moon lying under the surface of a permanently shadowed crater. The presence of significant water on the moon is critical for future lunar exploration. To check for water, LCROSS dropped a spent rocket booster into a lunar crater, sending a plume of dust into

Preparing Science Teaching Candidates 137

iSTEM Curriculum Framework Tool	
NGSS Expected Proficiencies • Develop a model that predicts and describes changes in particle motion, temperature, and state of a pure substance when thermal energy is added or removed (MS-PS1-4) • Collect data to provide evidence for how the motions and complex interactions of air masses results in changes in weather conditions (MS-ESS2-5).	
Phenomenon	**Relevant Conceptual Models**
During winter in Oregon, warm, moist unstable fronts from the Pacific Ocean mix with cold, dry, stable continental air masses, creating conditions for low-elevation Willamette Valley snow	Warm Air / Cold Air
Evidence-Based Argumentation Assessment Prompt • What do you think will happen when a warm, moist air mass meets a cold, dry air mass? How do you know this? Explain.	
What Language Would You Like Your Students To Use?	
Proficient Language Target: *I predict that clouds and precipitation will occur, because data show the pattern that rain and snow is more likely to happen in areas where warm, ocean air had moved inland and mixed with colder, dryer air. This is consistent with the kinetic model that predicts that when faster-moving warm water vapor molecules slow, they tend to adhere around dust and ice particles, condensing into liquid water droplets, which form clouds and possibly precipitation.*	**Emergent Language Target**: *I predict that clouds and precipitation will occur, because when a warm storm comes in from the coast and meets cold air in the valley it produces rain and snow. This is because when warm, moist air cools, the water molecules slow and condense into clouds.*
Language Forms and Functions Sequence of Events Description Explanation Cause and Effect Evidence-based argument	**Language Stems** The data show that first _____, then _____, and then _____. Over time, the data show that _____. For example, _____. Data that do not fit this pattern includes _____.

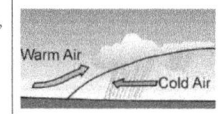

Academic Vocabulary	Science Vocabulary	
Predict	Collided	This is consistent with _____, that predicts when _____, _____ happens, causing _____.
Data	Kinetic model	
Pattern	Molecules	I predict that _____, because the data show _____.
Adhere	Condensation	
Mix	Precipitation	
	Vapor	
	Stability	

Figure 8.4 iSTEM literacy planning tool. *Source*: author created.

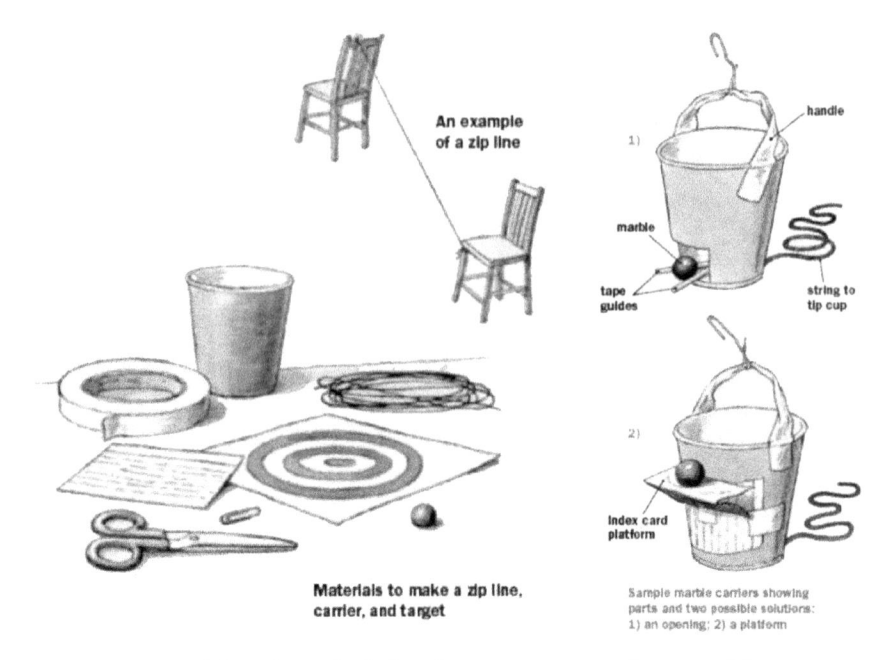

Figure 8.5 Materials and sample designs from *On Target* teacher materials.
Source: author created.

space. LCROSS sensors, positioned to take advantage of solar backlighting, scanned the resulting dust plume to detect the presence of water.

On Target challenges students with a similar task: Create a device to drop a marble from a moving paper cup onto a sand target crater. Students are supplied with string, cups, tape, paper clips, a marble, and a pie plate filled with sand. The cup slides down an inclined "zip line" for approximately 10 feet before the point at which the marble is released (figure 8.5). The goal is to create a design that is accurate, consistent, and replicable.

On Target provides a rich opportunity for students to work toward NGSS-expected proficiencies in engineering design (figure 8.6). *On Target* was implemented by a group of teacher–candidates and mentor teachers in a fifth-grade, dual-language classroom. Twenty-four students first explored LCROSS and the *On Target* challenge by discussing the question: "What supplies would we need in order to live on the moon?"

Students brainstormed a list of supplies such as shelter, fuel, food, water, and so on. Students were told that transporting items to space is expensive, so they would want to use supplies found on the moon as often as possible. Water is a necessity and common in the solar system, but it is heavy and expensive to transport to space. The students then viewed a NASA video designed to orient students to the goal of LCROSS (to find water on the moon) and to the main

Preparing Science Teaching Candidates 139

iSTEM Literacy Planning Tool Applied to *On Target*

NGSS Expected Proficiencies

- Define a simple design problem reflecting a need or a want that includes specified criteria for success and constraints on materials, time, or cost. (3-5-ETS1-1)
- Generate and compare multiple possible solutions to a problem based on how well each is likely to meet the criteria and constraints of the problem. (3-5-ETS1-2)
- Plan and carry out fair tests in which variables are controlled and failure points are considered to identify aspects of a model or prototype that can be improved. (3-5-ETS1-3)

Phenomenon	Relevant Conceptual Models
LCROSS drops rocket booster from a moving orbiter onto a desired target site on the moon	

Assessment Prompts

1. What problem are you trying to solve with your design? Include the criteria and constraints.
2. How did you use the materials to solve the problem?
3. Which parts of your solution worked? Which did not work? What did you try in order to improve your design?

What Language Would You Like Your Students To Use?

Proficient Language Target:	Emergent Language Target:
The problem was to design a craft to launch a marble onto a target while sliding down a string. We were constrained to using a paper cup, tape, string, and wire. The marble had to hit the target at least two out of three tries to meet the criteria for success.	We tried to make a ship to launch a marble onto a target. We had to use a paper cup, tape, string, and wire. We had to hit a target two out of three times.
First, a loop of wire was taped onto the cup so that it slid easily down the string. Then, a small hole was cut in the cup that the marble would go through if pushed hard. Finally, a string was tied to the cup so that it would stop and launch the marble onto the target.	We made a loop of wire and taped it onto the cup and we cut a small hole so the marble would come out. We tied a string onto the cup to make it stop at the right time
When our prototype was tested, it was found that the cup slid well down the string, but it failed because the marble got stuck in the hole when the cup stopped. We redesigned our prototype by making the hole bigger, and using tape to hold the marble steady. The next time we tested the design it almost hit the target. To improve the design further, we adjusted the string, and we met the criteria by hitting the target all three times.	The cup worked right on the string but the marble got stuck so we cut the hole bigger. We had to use tape to hold the marble, and it worked.

Language Forms and Functions		Language Stems
Description	Making Predictions	
Sequence	Persuading	The problem was _____.
Evaluation		We were constrained to using _____.

Academic Vocabulary	Science Vocabulary
problem	prototype, criteria, constraint,
design	failure

_____ to meet the criteria.

First, _____. Then, _____. Finally, _____.

When our prototype was tested, _____.

It failed because _____.

Figure 8.6 iSTEM literacy planning tool applied to *On Target*. *Source*: author created.

components of the LCROSS mission. The introductory lesson "frontloaded" vocabulary (e.g., force, weight, energy, mass, gravity, trajectory) necessary to support later student practice in speaking and writing about the project.

In the lesson's second session, students worked in small groups of three to four on the *On Target* design challenge. Students spent more than an hour brainstorming, creating, testing, and refining possible solutions, while teachers circulated among the groups, helping them to clarify their own ideas and theories. Each group demonstrated and explained to the whole group how they came to their final solution. Afterward, students wrote in their "science journals" about the design challenge, creating diagrams and using complete sentences to explain how they solved the problem, what challenges they had, and what questions remained (figure 8.7).

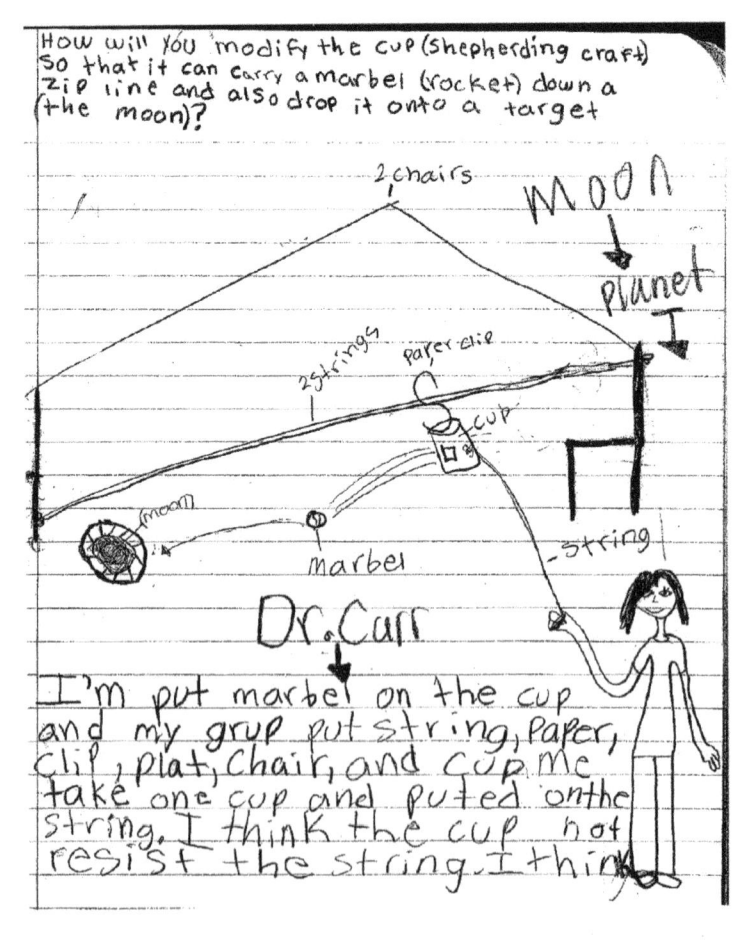

Figure 8.7 Sample *On Target* student work. *Source*: author created.

Practicing Academic Language

To document student-language practice, we collected written journal entries and videotaped student conversation. Besides using STEM vocabulary, students also practiced key language functions common to STEM academic text and speech. *On Target* motivated students to use a number of language functions in both speech and writing, allowing teachers to document and diagnose language usage (table 8.1). Teachers were able to intervene verbally in real time and in post-writing conferences with students.

The implementation of *On Target* in the fifth-grade classroom demonstrated some of the ways an engineering-design project may be used as a focused space within which language-development and science content may be seamlessly integrated. The project followed the general outline of many in-class engineering-design challenges, which feature a clear goal and criteria for

Table 8.1 Language Functions and Emergent Student Writing

Fluency-Building Activities in iSTEM	*Language Functions*	*Sample Student Writing and Speaking**
Define Problems	Defining	• "My experiment was to make the marble to the sand because were doing a experiment about outer space."
Testing and Refining Solution	Describing	• "I'm put marbel on the cup and my grup put string, paper, clip, plat, chair, and Cup me take one cup and puted on the string."
	Drawing Conclusions	• "At first I tried it and I missed because I did not pulled the string." • "I got an idea when I took this off (points) and it worked."
Communicate and Apply New Innovation	Retelling	• "When we tried to land the marble in the plate of sand. I tryed it more than 3 times but it didn't work." • "One problem we had to solve was aim at the middle and make it work." • "I thought of puting string half way on the cup, then when it was half way I pulled it and fell into the moon."
	Cause and Effect	• "I made it too much hole I think that's why it didn't work."

*"Corrections" above are based on this concept. Errors are intentional.

measuring success, constraints in the form of limited materials and time, and the opportunity for students to design and test prototypes. *On Target* was made literacy rich through intentionally frontloading literacy instruction with a focus on academic vocabulary and language functions used in STEM disciplines.

Teachers devoted significant time not only to analyzing student understanding of key engineering concepts such as prototype, criteria, constraint, and failure but also to the way students worked to use academic language functions and vocabulary. Mentor teachers observed that students were more engaged in literacy work during *On Target* than during typical literacy instruction, which is often driven by text materials rather that hands-on, challenging STEM projects.

DISCUSSION:
Sounding Smart

Literacy-rich science lessons and units can be designed and tested effectively by preservice teachers in collaboration with mentor teachers and university staff. Teams have been both challenged and rewarded by the step of constructing expected target responses to assessment prompts. By envisioning the kinds of "smart language" we desire to hear from students, we have realized that we have given too little consideration to the complexity of "sounding smart" in science, and we still suspect that time spent in class developing language is time taken away from building conceptual understanding. As a corrective measure, we have integrated the smart-language step into lesson and activity construction, even when time for planning is too short for a thorough consideration of language goals, forms, and functions.

For example, consider the following prompt, given to students in a high-school earth-science class, based on NGSS MS-ESS1-2. *Develop and use a model to describe the role of gravity in the motions within galaxies and the solar system.*

> NGSS Prompt: *(1) Collect data about the number of days between vernal and autumnal equinoxes through the year; (2) use the data to test and modify the circular model of the Earth's orbit around the Sun to account for the data; and (3) use the idea of gravity to explain changes in the motion of the Earth around the Sun during the year.*

Students used a calendar to "discover" that there are 186 days between the vernal equinox (March 21) and autumnal equinox (September 21) passing through summer, but 179 days between the vernal and fall equinoxes, passing through winter. The observation that there is a "long half" and "short half" of the year is puzzling given the model of a circular Earth orbit, which predicts equal numbers of days between equinoxes. Students can easily modify the circular model so that earth orbits in a slightly elliptical shape, in which the earth is slightly closer to the sun and faster-orbiting during the "short half" of the year, and slightly farther away and slower-orbiting during the long half.

The change in the Earth's orbital speed can be explained qualitatively by noting that the Sun exerts a stronger gravitational force when the Earth is closer, accelerating the Earth.

> Smart-Sounding Response: *Data about the yearly equinoxes showed that the summer period between equinoxes is longer than the winter period between equinoxes. This observation does not support the hypothesis made using the circular model of the Earth's orbit, which predicts equal times between equinoxes. The observation can be accounted for by modifying the circular model so that Earth orbits in a slight ellipse, so that it is slightly closer to the Sun during the winter half of the year and slightly farther during the summer half. The new model predicts that the Earth would travel faster around the Sun during the winter half because it is closer to the Sun and would experience a stronger gravitational pull.*

A smart-sounding response to the prompt involves a series of complex, linked sentences, written in passive voice:

- Data about _____ showed that _____.
- This observation does (does not) account for the hypothesis made using the _____ model, which predicts _____.
- The observation can be accounted for by modifying the model _____.
- The new model predicts that _____ because _____.

These sentence frames can be displayed as scaffolds for students to use when writing or speaking their responses to the prompt. Beyond simply sounding smart, constructing a response in academic language embeds the core scientific processes of data collection, hypothesis testing, and modeling. When student writing and speaking is scaffolded using sentence structures as shown, they are supported not only in learning to sound smart in science (which is critical), but in development of science concepts.

In simply drafting, redrafting, and examining the written and spoken responses we expect from students, it becomes clear that the task is often much more complex than we may realize and is, in fact, difficult to complete well, even by teachers who are content experts. Not surprisingly, the drafting and redrafting process results in deeper understanding even for content experts, revealing that the explicit scaffolding of language embedded in content instruction is an untapped resource for developing conceptual understanding.

CONCLUSION

On Target and other NGSS-driven curricula immerse ELL students in the kinds of rich activities that engage ELLs and other students in the types of purposeful, meaning-making activities known to facilitate academic language development (Kovach & Botello, 2011). Still, we are troubled by the fact that most students performed at only an emergent level when responding to NGSS-based assessment prompts.

Development of academic language requires the opportunity for students to speak, listen to, read, and write academic language in real contexts; iSTEM instruction provides these opportunities but must be sustained over time. Devoting significant time and resources to implementing literacy-rich science curricula during STEM teacher preparation may serve candidates to better meet the needs of students in high-needs settings, particularly where the acquisition of academic language for STEM is a focus.

NOTE

1. This research was supported by National Science Foundation Grants DUE-0934599 and DUE-1439628.

REFERENCES

Alberts, B. (2010). Prioritizing science education. *Science, 328*, 405.
Anders, P. (2012). The tools you need: Reading and writing processes and practices. Paper Presented at The Western Regional Noyce Conference. Tucson, AZ, November 17.
Common Core State Standards Initiative. (2015). Common Core State Standards. Retrieved May 1, 2015, from http://www.corestandards.org.
Cummins, J. (2001). *Negotiating Identities: Education for Empowerment in a Diverse Society*, third edition. Los Angeles, CA: California Association for Bilingual Education.
Darling-Hammond, L. (2010). *The flat world and education: How America's commitment to equity will determine our future*. New York: Teachers College Press.

ELPA21, (2014). *English* language proficiency assessment for the 21st century. Retrieved May 1, 2015, from http://www.elpa21.org.

Gee, J. P. (2004). Language in the science classroom: Academic social languages as the heart of school-based literacy. In E. W. Saul (Ed.), *Crossing borders in literacy and science instruction: Perspectives on theory and practice* (pp. 13–32). Arlington, VA: NSTA Press.

Gee, J. P. (2008).What is academic language? In A. S. Rosebery & B. Warren (Eds.), *Teaching science to English language learners* (pp. 57–71). Arlington, VA: NSTA Press.

Kim, C., Carr, K., & Pope, J. (2014). *Academic language activities in sheltered STEM content instruction*. Paper Presented at The Oregon Confederation of School Administrators State English Learners Alliance Conference. Eugene, OR, March 11.

Kovach, G., & Botello, R. (2011). Chicago teachers working to establish collaborative endeavors and partnerships for reforming and transforming STEM education for Els. Paper presented at the US Department of Education High-Quality STEM Education for English Learners: Current challenges and effective practices forum. Washington, DC, June 11.

Mccoss-Yergian, T., & Krepps, L. (2010) Do teacher attitudes impact literacy strategy implementation in content area classrooms? *Journal of Instructional Pedagogies, 4*. Retrieved February 23, 2012, from http://www.aabri.com/manuscripts/10519.pdf

National Research Council (NRC). (2011). *A framework for K–12 science education: Practices, crosscutting concepts, and core ideas*. Washington DC: National Academies Press.

Organisation for Economic Co-Operation and Development (OECD). (2012). OECD Programme for International Student Assessment (PISA). Retrieved February 18, 2012, from http://www.pisa.oecd.org.

President's Council of Advisors On Science and Technology (PCAST). (2010). Prepare and inspire: K–12 science, technology, engineering, and math (STEM) education for America's future. Retrieved November 29, 2018, from https://obamawhitehouse.archives.gov/sites/default/files/microsites/ostp/pcast-stem-ed-final.pdf.

Snow, C. E. (2010). Academic language and the challenge of reading for learning about science. *Science, 328*, 450–452.

Rodriguez, C. (2012). The research question, data collection, and evaluation plans for MSP targeted partnerships. Paper Presented at The Math and Science Partnerships (MSP) Proposal Development Workshop. Baltimore, MD, January 20–21.

Webb, P. (2010). Science education and literacy: Imperatives for the developed and developing world. *Science, 328*, 448–450.

Chapter 9

Promoting an Interdisciplinary Approach to STEM Education

Matching STEM Pedagogy to Trends on the Demand Side

Joseph Mukuni

The rationale for promoting an interdisciplinary approach to science, technology, engineering, and math (STEM) education has been indisputable in the conversations about STEM signature pedagogies primarily because, as Jenlink (2015, p. 203) points out, "The real world is not neatly divided into separate disciplines, and certainly imagining and realizing the future of education, democracy, and humanity is not reliant upon a singular disciplinary perspective, so why should STEM education be?" As a matter of fact, the justification for an interdisciplinary approach to education in general is an issue that has been well argued since the turn of the twentieth century, long before the concept of STEM came into vogue (see, e.g., Drake & Burns, 2004; Badley, 2009; Vars, 1991).

Vars (1991) reported that this discussion could be traced to as far back as the eighteen hundreds in the writing of Herbert Spencer. Badley (2009) (in an article interestingly titled "Resisting curriculum integration: Do good fences make good neighbors?") collaborated this long history when he reported:

> Curriculum integration has enjoyed a long history. The 1895 annual meeting of the National Herbart Society (in America now the National Society for the Study of Education or NSSE) focused on conceptions of curriculum meant to help students gain a coherent understanding of the world (Wraga, 1996). That meeting's focus served as only one part of an extended debate among educators of the time, a debate conducted on more than one continent. (p. 113)

Clearly, scholars have demonstrated the pedagogical value of adopting an interdisciplinary approach to education in general for several decades, and lately the debate has gotten even louder with special reference to STEM education. However, what appears to have received insufficient attention in the narrative of the interdisciplinarity of STEM education is the discussion about the evidence from the demand side.

Specifically, the evidence supporting the need for future STEM workers to be exposed to interdisciplinary approaches to work-related problem solving. Given that the major market for STEM talent is the world of work, it is prudent to pay close attention to trends in the labor market, which support the use of interdisciplinary approaches in processes concerned with the preparation of STEM talent.

This chapter, therefore, discusses how trends in the world of work justify the call for teachers and teacher educators to maintain a steady focus on pedagogies that promote interdisciplinary approaches to STEM education.

THE ECONOMIC MISSION OF STEM

In making a case for aligning STEM pedagogy to labor market trends, we need to bear in mind that one of the major reasons driving the reform in STEM education has been the nation's economic competiveness. In the 1980s, there were two main factors driving educational reform as identified by the American Association for the Advancement of Science, Project 2061 (1989). One of the concerns was that the affluence and international power of the United States were declining in relation to other countries such as Japan.

The second concern was that US public education was characterized by low test scores, students' avoidance of science and mathematics, a demoralized and weakening teaching staff, low learning expectations, and poor international ranking of students' knowledge of science and math. These concerns raised in the 1980s are somewhat similar to the reasons being given for the STEM educational reform today. According to the Executive Summary of the STEM National Action Plan:

> Business and industry leaders, governors, policy makers, educators, higher education officials, and our national defense and security agencies have repeatedly stated the need for efforts to reform the teaching of STEM disciplines in the Nation so that the United States will continue to be competitive in the global, knowledge-based economy. (National Science Foundation, 2007, p. 2)

The National Action Plan has noted that although the national crises have been the same over the last twenty-five years, recommendations made by various well-received reports have not been appropriately recognized and fully implemented. In explaining the context of the Action Plan, the National Science Foundation observed that students in the United States were not receiving the STEM education necessary for them to be effective participants in the knowledge-based economy.

One indicator of the problem was the number of students that had to do remedial work in science and mathematics to help them cope with college course work. The other indicator was that the United States tended to be close to the bottom of the performance rankings on international assessments such as the Programme for International Student Assessment (PISA) tests.

It is clear, therefore, that the overall goal of STEM education is to enable the United States to continue to be competitive in the global knowledge-based economy because it takes a good foundation of STEM disciplines in the school system (National Science Foundation, 2007, p. 2) for the nation to remain competitive.

CULTURE OF INTERDISCIPLINARY TEAMS IN WORKPLACES

Given that one major driver of the STEM reform is economic competitiveness, it is important that STEM educators pay attention to workplace trends and align STEM pedagogies to those trends. One of the organizational features of workplaces is the phenomenon of interdisciplinary teams (Taajamaa et al., 2014; Terpenny, Goff, Vernon, & Green, 2006; DeChurch & Mesmer-Magnus, 2010). The complexity of today's work (especially in engineering and with advancements in technology) demands an interdisciplinary approach.

As Heinendirk and Cadez (2013) have pointed out with particular reference to civil-engineering projects, graduates of STEM-related educational programs work together in interdisciplinary teams in the planning and execution of their work. For graduates of STEM-related programs to function in their workplaces, there is need for schools and institutions of higher learning to place due emphases on skills that facilitate teamwork and to help students to develop both disciplinary and interdisciplinary expertise. According to Golding (2009):

> Interdisciplinary education must supplement disciplinary teaching and learning so students can learn how to respond to challenges that transcend disciplines, work in the confluence of multiple disciplines, and develop research trajectories that do not conform to standard disciplinary paths. Interdisciplinary subjects are pivotal for this interdisciplinary education, teaching how to understand, navigate and employ multiple and often contrary ways of knowing. In these subjects students develop a meta-knowledge about different disciplines, methods and epistemologies, and learn how to purposefully and reflectively integrate and synthesize different perspectives in order to advance understanding and solve problems. (p. 2)

Apart from enabling students to be aware of the existence of different ways of knowing and the need to synthesize varying perspectives, development of interdisciplinary expertise will, inter alia, enable students to identify connections between and among different disciplines and (as a result) make them appreciate the importance of interdisciplinary teamwork. Appreciating the importance of interdisciplinary teams is as critical as the competencies required to function in a team because it is a key motivational factor for wanting to develop the teamwork skills.

Pedagogical Implications of Interdisciplinary Teams and Relevance to STEM Education

With so much said about the value of interdisciplinary teams in organizations' economic competiveness, it is suggested that institutions involved in STEM education should place greater emphasis than they do now on pedagogical approaches that promote teamwork. The rationale is that if interdisciplinary teams are an important feature of the sociopolitical landscape of workplaces, then STEM talent preparation in the entire pipeline from kindergarten to higher education should place due emphases on groupwork methodologies of learning.

Workforce development practitioners need not look too far to find learning theories on which to base groupwork methodologies that will prepare students for their future roles as participants in interdisciplinary teams at workplaces. Groupwork methodologies are grounded in the social constructivist theory of learning. This learning theory is associated with Lev Vygotsky (1896–1934), a Russian psychologist, who

> argued and presented evidence that the cognitive skills of human children are shaped by, or in some cases even created by, their interactions with others in the culture or with the artifacts and symbols that others have created for communal use. (Moll & Tomasello, 2007, p. 639)

The suggestion that is made, that STEM talent development systems should lay more emphasis on teamwork methodologies, is in accord with labor market demand. Many authors have indicated that employers are raising concerns that labor market entrants today lack employability skills, which include groupwork skills (Collet, Hine, & du Plessis, 2015; Lavy & Yadin, 2013; Bailey, Sass, Swiercz, Seal, & Kayes, 2005).

Bailey et al. (2005), for instance, observed that "[b]usiness leaders have voiced concern that fresh recruits remain ill equipped for the group dynamics of decentralized organizations. Although technically proficient, new employees display limited self-awareness, leadership, interpersonal communication, and conflict management skills" (p. 40). This justifies the suggestion that schools and colleges should put more emphases than they do now on methodologies that enable learners to develop teamwork skills.

The skills that students need to develop to participate effectively in interdisciplinary teams include interpersonal skills (e.g., team spirit, flexibility, integrity, accountability); thinking skills (e.g., decision making, creativity, problem solving); and communication skills (e.g., listening, empathy, clarity, negotiation).

To teach these skills, it will help if teachers use strategies that enable students to learn by doing, that is, to work in groups in solving real-world problems that will engage them authentically and make them develop higher-order thinking skills (McCormick, 2004). It will also help if teachers themselves work as teams through team-teaching and through joint assessment of students' learning, instead of working in silos.

As I have indicated elsewhere (Mukuni, 2015), the interdisciplinary approach to STEM education will not just happen. It will take the development of a sustainable enabling environment that supports collaboration at three levels; namely, planning, instruction, and reflection (Brown & Smith, 1997). Planning entails joint preparation of lessons by experienced and new teachers together. Collaboration at the instruction stage could take the form of team teaching. During the reflection stage, the interdisciplinary team of teachers evaluate lessons to determine what worked, what needed modification, and what could be added or avoided next time.

Interdisciplinary collaboration seems to be an obvious way of approaching STEM education. However, it will be effective only if, as Shulman (1993) says, teaching is transformed from private to community property and teachers begin to learn from each other's signature pedagogies. This is, of course, asking teachers to make a paradigm shift from having teaching as a private affair to making it community property. There is a lot that teachers can learn from colleagues in different disciplines, but there is likely to be much resistance, as Shulman admits.

However, as Nespor (1987) has pointed out, if we want to understand (and perhaps influence) the way teachers do what they do, we need to pay attention to their beliefs and the goals they pursue. What they learn or refuse to learn about making teaching community property (or about changing pedagogies) is a function of their beliefs. A personal belief is that it is harder to educate people's hearts than it is to educate their minds and hands.

One African adage is that what cuts down a tree is not the sharpness of the axe, but the heart of the person cutting the tree. A heart that believes that an axe is blunt will not cut a tree, despite the fact that the axe is actually sharp. In the same way, a heart that is convinced that interdisciplinary collaboration does not add any value to STEM pedagogy will lead to discouragement of any effort toward team teaching or interdisciplinary collaboration.

An Approach to Interdisciplinary Integration of Curriculum

A useful starting point for developing an interdisciplinary approach to STEM education is interdisciplinary integrative curriculum design. Drake and Burns (2004) suggested a framework for classifying forms of integration into three types, namely: multidisciplinary, interdisciplinary, and transdisciplinary.

The approach presented by Drake and Burns (2004) provides a useful guide for designing an integrative curriculum. First, Drake and Burns have given a step-by-step procedure for designing an integrative curriculum (starting with scanning and clustering of standards and ending with instructional and assessment strategies). Second, they have exemplified the approach through the use of diagrams, taking the theme of medieval times to illustrate how science, language arts, social studies, and arts can be intentionally integrated through this approach.

This approach is not specifically meant for technological and engineering design-based lessons. However, it can be used for that purpose by careful selection of a guiding question that requires students to engage in a problem-solution activity that typifies engineering design-based lessons.

The guiding question would pose a problem, require students to search for possible solutions, develop and test a prototype, and present their product for peer assessment (or teacher assessment). This approach takes care of the problem of a teacher's inability to address content from more than one STEM discipline because the first step provides for the selection of broad-based standards for each discipline.

This scanning and clustering of standards need not be done by a single teacher. A teacher who is not comfortable with the content of other disciplines can work with specialists in those disciplines. Similarly, the instruction (which could take the form of student-teacher or student-student consultations) and assessment can be done in collaboration with other teachers and students. Teaching STEM content through this approach would be effective because it would ensure fidelity (if students are made to engage in authentic problem-solving activities and are provided context for both the content and practice of the STEM disciplines), and learning would be more meaningful and enjoyable.

Toward Interdisciplinary Problem-Based Learning in Teacher Preparation

On the demand side of the STEM pipeline, there is unanimity among employers and workers that two of the key soft skills that students must have in preparation for employment are teamwork and problem solving (Crawford & Dalton, 2016; Vaz & Quinn, 2015; Abdulwahed, Balid, Hasna, & Pokharel, 2013). Reporting on a recent survey carried out among engineering graduates in the industry, Vaz and Quinn (2015) say:

The alumni, who ranged over a span of 38 years' worth of graduates, reported long term gains in independent learning, problem-solving, project management, leadership, teamwork, oral and written communication, and global awareness as a result of their project work, and also described personal impacts such as character development, self-efficacy, and confidence development. (p. 3)

For students in STEM-based programs to be familiar with and competent in these soft skills, the teachers that prepare them for their future roles in STEM-related fields should adopt methodologies that foster development of these skills. One such methodology is the problem-based learning (PBL) approach. By its nature, the PBL approach shifts the burden of learning from the teacher to the student.

The teacher, in PBL, is no longer playing the traditional role of a didactic dispenser of knowledge but a facilitator of learning. The literature on the subject of PBL (see, e.g., Savery, 2006; Walker & Leary, 2009; Hung, 2011; Barrows, 2002) describes these changed roles in the classroom.

The teacher's roles include creating learning situations in which students are engaged in developing answers to real-world problems; coming up with real-world ambiguous problems that challenge students' critical-thinking skills; ensuring that the nature of the problem is multidisciplinary (which entails interdisciplinary collaboration among teachers from the planning stage through the implementation stage up to assessment of student performance); monitoring the learning process with a view to providing scaffolding where needed; giving feedback to students; and evaluating the outcomes of learning for purposes of maintaining records of students' achievements and challenges.

For their part, students (preferably in interdisciplinary pairs or groups of three to five) negotiate among themselves the meaning of the problem with which the teacher has challenged them; jointly develop strategies for approaching the problem; create knowledge from available human and nonhuman resources and from their experiences; seek feedback from colleagues and from faculty; and transfer knowledge gained from solving a problem to similar problems.

As indicated, the learning situation described requires teachers of different disciplines to work together. They will need to agree on the rationale for working together and then plan together how they will implement the PBL within the constraints of time, differences in teaching philosophies, possible inadequate support from school administrators, varying standards of their subject matter, limited resources, challenges of group dynamics, and so on. They will also need to agree on when to go solo and when to work together.

It is common knowledge among teachers that we teach according to how we were taught. It will, therefore, be necessary that faculty in teacher-preparation programs practice interdisciplinary PBL. That way, student teachers will gain experiential knowledge of the pedagogical benefit of collaborative learning, experimentation, and adaptation to suit realities of ambiguous situations. Faculty in teacher-preparation programs should create opportunities for interdisciplinary collaboration and adopt PBL. They should also require their students to demonstrate knowledge of this approach to teaching STEM when they go out for their student-teaching internships in schools.

CONCLUSION

Conversations about interdisciplinary approaches to learning and teaching, or curriculum integration, have been going on for ages. In recent years, discussions about this subject have gained momentum with the attention being given to STEM education. Educators and researchers have demonstrated the pedagogical value of adopting an interdisciplinary approach to STEM education.

The contribution of this chapter to the narrative on the interdisciplinary approach to STEM pedagogy is that in addition to the reasons that have so far been given to justify interdisciplinary approaches to STEM education, trends in the labor market point to the need for students to learn how to function in interdisciplinary teams. Classrooms where future workers in STEM fields are prepared should foster methodologies that promote interdisciplinary approaches to problem solving, simulating authentic contexts in which STEM-related knowledge, skills, and attitudes will be applied in the real world beyond the classroom. Against this background, it is only prudent that teacher educators prepare future teachers for their role of managing interdisciplinary learning situations.

REFERENCES

Abdulwahed, M., Balid, W., Hasna, M.O., & Pokharel, S. (2013). Skills of engineers in knowledge-based economies: A comprehensive literature review. 2013 IEEE International Conference on Teaching, Assessment and Learning for Engineering (TALE). Retrieved November 29, 2018, from http://ieeexplore.ieee.org/stamp/stamp.jsp?arnumber=6654540.

American Association for the Advancement of Science, Project 2061. (1989). *Science for All Americans.* Retrieved November 29, 2018, from http://www.project2061.org/publications/sfaa/online/sfaatoc.htm.

Bailey, J., Sass, M., Swiercz, P. M., Seal, C., & Kayes, D. C. (2005). Teaching with and through teams: Student-written, instructor-facilitated case writing and the signatory code. *Journal of Management Education, 29*(1), 39–59. Retrieved May 1, 2012, from abi/inform global. (document id: 923585531).

Barrows, H. S. (2002). Is it truly possible to have such a thing as DPBL? *Distance Education, 23*(1), 119–122.

Bradley, K. (2009). Resisting curriculum: Do good fences make good neighbors? *Issues in Integrative Studies, 27*, 113–137.

Brown, C. A., & Smith, M. S. (1997). Supporting the development of mathematical pedagogy. *Mathematics Teacher, 90*(2), 138–143.

Collet, C., Hine, D., & Du Plessis, K. (2015) Employability skills: Perspectives from a knowledge-intensive industry. *Education and Training, 57*(5), 532–559. doi: 10.1108/ET-07-2014-0076.

Crawford, P., & Dalton, R. (2016). Providing built environment students with the necessary skills for employment: Finding the required soft skills. *Current Urban Studies, 4*(1), 97–123. doi: 10.4236/Cus.2016.41008.

Dechurch, L. A., & Mesmer-Magnus, J. R. (2010). The cognitive underpinnings of effective teamwork: A meta-analysis. *Journal of Applied Psychology, 95*(1), 32–53. doi: 10.1037/A0017328.

Drake, S., & Burns, R. (2004). *Meeting standards through integrated curriculum.* Alexandria, VA: ASCD.

Golding, C. (2009). *Integrating the disciplines: Successful interdisciplinary subjects.* Melbourne, Australia: Center for the Study of Higher Education.

Heinendirk, E., & Cadez, I. (2013). Innovative teaching in civil engineering with disciplinary teamwork. organization, technology and management in construction. *An International Journal, 5*(2), 874–880. Retrieved November 29, 2018, from http://www.grad.hr/otmcj/clanci/vol5_is2/6.pdf.

Hung, W. (2011). Theory to reality: A few issues in implementing problem-based learning. *Education Tech Research Development* (59), 529–552.

Jenlink, P. M. (2015). STEM teacher education—Imagining a metadisciplinary future [editorial]. *Teacher Education and Practice, 28*(2/3), 197–207.

Lavy, I., & Yadin, A. (2013). Soft skills—An important key for employability in the 'shift to a service driven economy' era. *International Journal of E-Education, E-Business, E-Management and E-Learning, 3*(5), 416–420. doi: 10.7763/ijeeee.2013.v3.270.

Mccormick, R. (2004). Issues of learning and knowledge in technology education. *International Journal of Technology and Design Education, 14*(1), 21–44.

Moll, H., & Tomasello, M. (2007). Cooperation and human cognition: The vygotskian intelligence hypothesis. *Philosophical Transactions of the Royal Society B, 362*(1480), 639–648.

Mukuni, J. (2015). The chronic shortage of STEM talent: The place of integrative STEM education. *Teacher Education and Practice, 28*(2/3), 208–220.

National Science Foundation. (2007). National action plan for addressing science, technology, engineering, and mathematics in education system. Retrieved November 29, 2018, from https://www.nsf.gov/pubs/2007/nsb07114/nsb07114.pdf.

Nespor, J. (1987). The role of beliefs in the practice of teaching. *Journal of Curriculum Studies, 19*(4), 317–328.

Savery, J. R. (2006). Overview of problem-based learning: Definitions and distinctions. *Interdisciplinary Journal of Problem-Based Learning, 1*(1), 9–20.

Shulman, L. (1993). *Teaching as community property.* Princeton, NJ: Carnegie Foundation for the Advancement of Teaching.

Taajamaa, V., Westerlund, T., Guo, X., Hupli, M., Salantera, S., & Salakoski, T. (2014). Interdisciplinary engineering education—Practice based case. Paper Presented at the Fourth Interdisciplinary Design Education Conference, IEEE: Santa Clara, CA, March 3. Retrieved November 29, 2018, from http://ieeexplore.ieee.org/stamp/stamp.jsp?arnumber=6784677.

Terpenny, J. P., Goff, R. M., Vernon, M. R., & Green, W. R. (2006). Utilizing assistive technology design projects and interdisciplinary teams to foster inquiry and learning in engineering design. *International Journal of Engineering Education, 22*(3), 609–616.

Vars, G. (1991). Integrated curricula in historical perspective. *Education Leadership, 49*(2), 14–15.

Vaz, R. F., & Quinn, P. (2015). Benefits of a project-based curriculum: Engineering employers' perspectives. Paper Presented at 122nd ASEE Annual Conference and Exposition. Seattle, WA, June 14–17. Retrieved November 29, 2018, from http://peer.asee.org/23617.

Walker, A., & Leary, H. (2009). A problem-based learning meta-analysis: Differences across problem types, implementation types, disciplines, and assessment levels. *Interdisciplinary Journal of Problem-Based Learning, 3*(1). Retrieved from https://doi.org/10.7771/1541-5015.1061.

Wraga, W. G. (1996). A century of interdisciplinary curricula in American schools. In P. S. Hlebowitsh & W. G. Wraga (Eds.), *Annual review of research for educational leaders* (pp. 117–145). New York: Scholastic/National Association of Secondary School Principals.

Chapter 10

Epilogue

The Future of STEM Teaching

Patrick M. Jenlink and Karen Embry Jenlink

What we know is that the future of teaching is both uncertain and shaped in part by our actions in the present. Advancing science, technology, engineering, and math (STEM) teacher preparation to an interdisciplinary[1] approach offers an opportunity for STEM teachers to develop different and necessary cognitive, epistemological, and sociocultural ways of understanding teaching and learning, and at the same time, develop different and heretofore undiscovered strategies needed to solve complex, interdisciplinary problems and gain skills and knowledge that the future will require (Ayar & Yalvac, 2016; Chettiparamb, 2007; Holley, 2017; Sahin, Ayar, & Adiguzel, 2014).

The generation of STEM teachers we prepare today will be responsible, in turn, for preparing a new generation of STEM education possibilities, and in turn, preparing a new generation of STEM-minded citizens, innovators, leaders, and teachers. This new generation of STEM teachers will be responsible for the education necessary to meet the challenges yet to be experienced as we move into the future.

TOWARD A NEW LEVEL OF THINKING

Although educators are aware of the importance of STEM education, neither educators nor researchers consistently agree on or understand what STEM education should really be about in K–12 education or what STEM teacher preparation should be about in terms of preparing teachers for teaching in and across the STEM disciplines. That said, it is important to note that in K–12 and higher-education settings, "STEM disciplines are taught in silos" (Wang, Moore, Roehrig, & Park, 2011, p. 2).

Why is this point important? For decades, we have taught not only STEM disciplines, but also, most, if not all, disciplines in silos. As education has evolved historically, we have tended to hold on to old ways. A quote often attributed to Albert Einstein suggests: "We cannot solve our problems with the same thinking we used when we created them."[2] So, where might we look to hear beyond the dominant understanding or language that disciplines what we know?

The importance of learning about other cultures resides in the need to not only understand ourselves as subjects, but also to gain consciousness of how we exercise or submit to power relations politically, economically, culturally, and educationally. This is as true for teacher preparation as it is for the public in general.

As the needs of our educational system have evolved, the utility of teaching STEM disciplines, or any disciplines for that matter, in silos has passed. To draw on Einstein once again, in "A Message to Intellectuals" ([1950] 2003) he stated:

> Our situation is not comparable to anything in the past. It is impossible, therefore, to apply methods and measures which at an earlier age might have been sufficient. We must revolutionize our thinking, revolutionize our actions, and must have the courage to revolutionize relations among the nations of the world. Clichés of yesterday will no long do today, and will, not doubt be hopelessly out of date tomorrow. (p. 52)

We live in a world that is far from "disciplinary," a world that involves making connections between disciplines,[3] between multiple areas of study authentically brought together through the circumstance of everyday life. In this sense, we live in a world that requires of us a perspective and understanding of the world that is greater than the sum of different disciplines, a world where it all comes together, both in the universal and the personal sense.

We can no longer reside safely in our disciplinary silos and meet the future. We must focus on integration of experiences and academics and perspectives toward the future of our youth. STEM education and teaching alone will not be sufficient for securing a future that is not a replica of the past, replete with the same complex array of problems that define the world and its educational systems today.

It is not enough to integrate the disciplines of science, technology, engineering, and math around a theme, common learnings, or a real-life context. Although this integration is important, if STEM teachers are to teach and enable students to develop awareness of "complex interdependencies and

[be] able to synthesize learning from a wide array of sources, to learn from experience, and to make productive connections between theory and practice" (Huber & Hutchings, 2005, p. 3), then teachers must be intentional in every aspect of who they are and what they do each day in classrooms. Preparing intentional educators will require that teacher education be intentional; intentionality means commitment to students, to the profession, and to the future.

STEPS FORWARD

Preparing teachers to enter classrooms to teach in and across STEM and non-STEM disciplines will require much work in rearticulating teacher preparation to align with the needs of a changing global society. The first step is to consider the historical nature of academic disciplines that dominate the current culture of academe. University faculty, STEM discipline faculty, and teacher-preparation faculty are "socialized to their respective disciplinary norms" (Holley, 2017, p. 1) over time and through their own academic experiences. Interdisciplinarity "is a complex endeavor" (1) that includes breaking down old cultural and disciplinary patterns and silos.

The second step forward to an interdisciplinary approach to STEM teacher preparation is to create communities of discourse to examine the lines of demarcation that separate the STEM disciplines, one from the other. Equally important is to examine the lines that separate STEM disciplines in the current teacher preparation programs.

The second step requires that STEM discipline and teacher-preparation faculty come together to "explore the varying and complex perceptions of interdisciplinary teaching and research faculty hold" (Lattuca, 2001, p. 405). Equally important is examining, together, how these perceptions may affect the process of interdisciplinary classroom interactions because faculty embrace different epistemological views of interdisciplinary curricula, pedagogy, and practice.

The third step is to answer the question as to whether we, as teacher educators, can strengthen teacher education's "claim to a coherent, cogent, deliberative and distinctive intellectual place by articulating the intersections and co-dependencies that constitute its interdisciplinarity?" (Kalantzis & Cope, 2014, p. 102).

STEM teaching and learning, envisioned as a set of actions and dispositions, is a broad, complex, and difficult area of inquiry and responsibility, "which by its very nature needs to be conceived in peculiarly interdisciplinary terms" (Kalantzis & Cope, 2014, p. 102). Interdisciplinary in the sense of bringing STEM disciplines together "is grounded in the historical practices of more than one discipline, and consciously crosses disciplinary contexts and boundaries" (p. 102).

The fourth step is to examine the place-based nature of problems that the STEM disciplines currently address in the workforce and in society, to examine the challenges that, at present, are not resolvable from within a singular disciplinary perspective and then advance an interdisciplinary approach that integrates the STEM disciplines and coordinates a place-based approach to clinical experiences. These clinical experiences should draw from real-world STEM problems that are authentic and necessitate teacher educators to create original and complex interdisciplinary paths to learning at an interdisciplinary level.

The fifth step is to recognize that once we take the first step toward an interdisciplinary approach to teacher preparation, there is no turning back; there is only moving toward the future. In recognizing the need for an interdisciplinary approach to STEM teacher preparation we must also recognize that teaching and research faculty have a responsibility to engage in interdisciplinary research that seeks to understand the nature and evolution of interdisciplinary STEM teaching.

This interdisciplinary research will serve the purpose of understanding the first four steps in the progression toward the future of STEM teacher preparation. Equally important, this research perspective will provide opportunities to advance beyond interdisciplinarity in STEM education and begin to explore options for not only understanding interdisciplinary STEM teaching but also to create a path to understanding of STEM education as metadisciplinary in nature (Kalantzis & Cope, 2014).

CONCLUSIONS

The time for disciplinary silos in education has passed; STEM education can no longer be situated within disciplinary silos any more than the preparing a new generation of STEM teachers can be situated in the past and present. As we move toward the future, we need to innovate teacher education to create an interdisciplinary educational system that invigorates learning and recognizes that learning is much larger than a classroom or the interactions with a teacher. Learning that is directed by interdisciplinary STEM is learning that embraces all the partners that make STEM possible, and at the same time, make STEM necessary to future of our nation.

NOTES

1. Interdisciplinary, in this case, means "integration of knowledge from multiple disciplines in pursuit of an outcome that is not possible from a single disciplinary approach. Interdisciplinary integration can occur through blending and linking different epistemological forms" (Holley, 2017, p. 4). Accordingly, interdisciplinary STEM teacher preparation and STEM teaching in classrooms refers to curriculum, pedagogy, and learning that draws on two or more disciplines and leads to an integration of disciplinary insights that otherwise would not be possible.

2. In an interview with Michael Amrine published in The *New York Times Magazine* in 1946, titled *The Real Problem is in the Hearts of Men*, Einstein, responding to a telegram sent out by a group of scientist organizations to prominent people seeking funding for "a new type of thinking" ([1946] 1960, p. 13) which was published in a previous issue of *The New York Times*, titled *Atomic Education Urged by Einstein*, explained: "Many persons have inquired concerning a recent message of mine that "a new type of thinking is essential if mankind is to survive and move to higher levels" (p. 7).

3. Kalantzis and Cope (2014) explained academic discipline as a "distinctive way of making knowledge . . . a field of deep and detailed content knowledge, a community of professional practice, a form of discourse (of fine semantic distinction and precise technicality), an area of work (such as an academic department or a research area), a domain of publication and public communication (p. 102).

REFERENCES

Ayar, M. C., & Yalvac, B. (2016). Lessons learned: Authenticity, interdisciplinarity, and mentoring for STEM learning environments. *International Journal of Education in Mathematics, Science and Technology*, 4(1), 30–43.

Chettiparamb, A. (2007). *Interdisciplinarity: A literature review*. Southampton, UK: The Interdisciplinary Teaching and Learning Group, Subject Centre For Languages, Linguistics and Area Studies, School of Humanities, University of Southampton.

Einstein, A. ([1946] 1960). The real problem is in the hearts of men. Interview by Michael Amrine. *New York Times,* Sunday Magazine, June 23, p. 7, reprinted in Otto Nathan & Heinz Norde (Eds.), *Einstein on peace* (pp. 383–388). New York: Schocken Books, 1960.

Einstein, A. ([1950] 2003). A message to intellectuals. In J. Green (Ed.), *Rebel lives* (pp. 49–56). New York: Ocean Press.

Holley, K. (2017). Interdisciplinary curriculum and learning in higher education. *Oxford research encyclopedia of education*. doi: 10.1093/acrefore/9780190264093.013.138.

Huber, M. T., & Hutchings, P. (2005). *Integrative learning: Mapping the terrain*. Washington, DC: Association of American Colleges and Universities.

Kalantzis, M., & Cope, B. (2014). Education is the new philosophy: To make a metadisciplinary claim for learning sciences. In A. D. Reid, P. E. Hart, &

M. A. Peters (Eds.), *A companion to research in education* (pp. 101–115). New York: Springer-Verlag.

Latuca, L. (2001). *Creating interdisciplinarity: Interdisciplinary research and teaching among college and university faculty.* Nashville, TN: Vanderbilt University Press.

Sahin, A., Ayar, M. C., & Adiguzel, T. (2014). STEM-related after-school program activities and associated outcomes on student learning. *Educational Sciences: Theory and Practice, 14*(1), 309–322.

Wang, H., Moore, T., Roehrig, G. H., & Park, Mi Sun. (2011). STEM integration: Teacher perceptions and practice. *Journal of Pre-College Engineering Education Research (J-PEER) 1*(2). Retrieved November 29, 2018, from http://dx.doi.org/10.5703/1288284314636.

About the Editors

Patrick M. Jenlink is Regents Professor, the E. J. Campbell Endowed Chair, professor of educational leadership, and professor of doctoral studies in the Department of Secondary Education and Educational Leadership at Stephen F. Austin State University in Nacogdoches, Texas. His experience for more than four decades as an educator includes STEM teaching with emphasis in biology I and II, chemistry, physics, and human anatomy and physiology, as well as serving as a building administrator, school district superintendent, professor at Western Michigan University, an evaluator and research consultant on National Science Foundation funded Statewide Systemic STEM initiative in Michigan, senior researcher on funded STEM initiatives in Oklahoma with NASA and Oklahoma State University, and senior researcher in a grant-funded STEM initiative in Texas, the *Texas State Middle Level Mathematics Project*. Jenlink's research interests include STEM literacy, meta-disciplinarity and pedagogy, educator preparation, STEM architecture, and leadership for STEM innovation. He has edited or authored twelve books and authored more than seventy book chapters. As well, he has authored and published 175 peer-refereed articles, and more than two hundred peer-refereed conference papers. Currently, Dr. Jenlink serves as editor of *Teacher Education & Practice* and as editor of *Scholar-Practitioner Quarterly*, both refereed journals.

Karen Embry Jenlink is professor of doctoral studies in educational leadership at Stephen F. Austin State University in Nacogdoches, Texas. Embry-Jenlink has directed or served on several initiatives to support STEM, educator preparation, and workforce development, including the Texas Middle Level State Mathematics Project, US Integrated Workforce Standards, Texas Regional Collaboratives for Excellence in Science and Mathematics, College and Career Readiness Mathematics Faculty Collaborative, and as PI/Co-PI of two Robert Noyce Scholarship Programs. Embry-Jenlink is an internationally renowned teacher educator and has collaborated on educational research in China, Costa Rica, Croatia, the Czech Republic, Hungary, England, Ireland, and Spain. She has published more than sixty-five peer-reviewed journal articles, book chapters, and technical reports and three books. In 2017, as national president of the Association of Teacher Educators, Embry Jenlink, appointed the ATE/NASA Education Commission on *STEM Education in the Future*. For her innovation and achievements in education, she has received several awards, including Outstanding Alumnus (TAMU-C 2005) and Honorary Life Member of Texas PTA for her service to public education in Texas (2014). She currently serves on the Board of Directors of the World Federation of the Association of Teacher Educators.

About the Contributors

Justin Boyle is assistant professor at the University of Alabama within the College of Education Department of Curriculum and Instruction. He is interested in how to improve the preparation of secondary mathematics teachers so that they can engage their students in communicating mathematical arguments. He recently coauthored a book titled *We Reason & We Prove for ALL Mathematics: Building Students Critical Thinking, Grades 6–12*.

Julie Bryant is an elementary school principal with the Bernalillo Public Schools in New Mexico. Previously, she had an appointment as assistant professor of education at Coker College where she focused her research and teaching on learning equity in early childhood education and literacy.

Kevin Carr is professor of education in the College of Education, Pacific University. He is also a regional leader in training current teachers in inquiry-based science teaching in Earth and space science, and he teaches an introductory astronomy in the Pacific University College of Arts and Sciences. His scholarly interests include preservice science teacher action research and science teacher professional development. Currently, he is Principal Investigator on *Pacific STEM Teaching Pathways*, a National Science Foundation Robert Noyce Scholarship Grant. Previously, he taught high school physics in Roseburg and Portland, Oregon, for seven years.

Jamie Collins is a Lecturer and the Secondary Graduate Education Field Experience Coordinator for the Department of Curriculum and Instruction at the University of Arkansas. Her research focuses on the ways in which early career teachers develop their identities, how English Language Arts is understood and taught in interdisciplinary and project-based learning settings, and the ways in which university courses discursively construct professional teacher preparation experiences.

Christa Jackson is assistant professor in mathematics education in the STEM Education Department at the University of Kentucky. She teaches undergraduate and graduate courses in mathematics education. Her research conceptualizes teachers' knowledge of equity, specifically in teaching mathematics to African American students. Her work focuses on effective mathematics instruction at the elementary and middle levels, strategies to help students who struggle in mathematics, and prospective mathematics teachers' conceptions of equity.

Ayesha Livingston graduated with her doctorate in educational psychology in May of 2018. She now lives in Charlottesville, VA where her research focuses on motivation and mathematics beliefs in preservice teachers. Additionally, she is researching structures that would allow a means to increase communication between researchers and practitioners in the classroom, enabling teachers to have access to viable research that has been translated to practice.

Margaret Mohr-Schroeder is associate professor of middle/secondary mathematics education in the STEM Education Department at the University of Kentucky, where she is the STEM Education and Secondary Mathematics Program Chair. Her research focuses on mathematics knowledge for teaching preservice and in-service teachers, especially conceptualizing innovative and research-based strategies for increasing this knowledge.

Deborah Moore-Russo is associate professor of mathematics education at the University at Buffalo. Moore-Russo studies teachers' reflections and their sense of obligation to the discipline of mathematics. She focuses on how mathematical concepts and ideas that involve mathematical concepts are modeled and communicated, often considering the role that technology plays in this process.

Joseph Mukuni earned his education specialist degree as well as a PhD in career and technical education at Virginia Tech. Before taking up studies at Virginia Tech, Mukuni had worked as a teacher educator in Zambia before rising to the position of national director responsible for both vocational training and technical education in the government of the Republic of Zambia. Currently, he is visiting assistant professor at Virginia Tech in career and technical education.

About the Contributors

Louis S. Nadelson is associate professor and director for the Center for the School of the Future in the Emma Eccles Jones College of Education at Utah State University. He has a BS from Colorado State University, a BA from the Evergreen State College, a MEd from Western Washington University, and a PhD in educational psychology from the University of Nevada, Las Vegas. His scholarly interests include all areas of STEM teaching and learning, inservice and preservice teacher professional development, program evaluation, multidisciplinary research, and conceptual change. Nadelson uses his more than twenty years of high school and college math, science, computer science, and engineering teaching to frame his research on STEM teaching and learning. Nadelson brings a unique perspective of research, bridging experience with practice and theory to explore a range of interests in STEM teaching and learning.

Jonathan Pope is adjunct instructor in STEM education, College of Education, Pacific University. He has taught bilingual elementary and middle school for more than thirty years and has co-directed professional development in STEM-language literacy.

D. Craig Schroeder holds dual BS degrees in physics and mathematics from Centre College, a MS and PhD in mathematics education, and an EdS in educational leadership from the University of Kentucky. He began teaching high school in Kentucky in 2002 and served as a middle-school mathematics coach for a grant project in Fayette County in 2011/2012. He is presently a middle-school mathematics and science teacher at Beaumont Middle School and director of the See Blue™ STEM Camp for middle-school students. His interests include using technology effectively in the mathematics and science classrooms, developing self-regulated learning, and helping students to explore and apply real-world STEM concepts in informal learning settings.

Anne L. Seifert is the Idaho National Laboratory STEM coordinator and founder and executive director of the i-STEM network. She holds a BS degree in elementary education, an MA in Education Administration, and an EDS in Educational Leadership. As a thirty-year veteran teacher and administrator she has been involved in school reform, assessment, literacy, student achievement, and school improvement. Her current work involves coordinating partnerships with educators, the Idaho Department of Education, business, and industry to raise STEM Education awareness. Seifert's research interests include STEM education, inquiry- and project-based instruction with the incorporation of twenty-first-century learning, change practices, and cultural influences on school effectiveness.

About the Contributors

Astrid Steele is assistant professor at the Schulich School of Education, Nipissing University, Canada, where she teaches science methods and works toward the development of scientific and environmental literacy. More than three decades of work as an educator, both in traditional-classroom settings and in alternative venues with diverse groups of students, informs her current research in the convergence of science, values and environmental teaching, and learning.

Abigail Stiles is a PhD student at the University of New Mexico in the department of Language, Literacy, and Sociocultural Studies. Abigail's research focuses on student literacy, teacher retention, and education policy. She is currently a Senior Fiscal Analyst for the New Mexico Legislative Education Study Committee, where she researches best practices around school climate and concerning charter school policy.

Vanessa Svihla is an associate professor at the University of New Mexico with appointments in the Organization, Information & Learning Sciences program and the Department of Chemical & Biological Engineering. As a learning scientist, her research focuses on how people learn as they design and teachers as designers of learning experiences. She received the NSF CAREER award to study ways to support students to develop agency over framing design problems, and the Spencer/National Academy of Education post doctoral fellowship to study design teaching and learning in a project based school.

Kersti Tyson is associate professor of Mathematics Education at the University of New Mexico. She is a learning scientist, mathematics educator and teacher educator. Her research focuses on teacher and learner listening. She is currently active in research projects that focus on improving children's opportunities to learn mathematics, especially for children from diverse backgrounds. With the PLUSS research team, funded by the Spencer Foundation, Kersti is developing a framework for Pedagogical Listening to describe the complex listening teachers do to support children to engage in rich mathematics discussions and learning opportunities.

Shawn Vecellio is a faculty member in the Teacher Education Department at The National Hispanic University (San Jose, CA). He teaches credential courses in foundations, field experience, diversity, and equity and also serves as master's thesis advisor to degree candidates. He has published articles in journals such as *Multicultural Perspectives* and *Schools: Studies in Education*. Since completing his dissertation on critical thinking, Vecellio has extended his research into the areas of social justice and integrating literature across the curriculum. In his teaching, he emphasizes reflective practice while using problem posing and essential questions to help educators develop their philosophy of teaching. His prior experience includes teaching at elementary-, middle-, and high-school (mathematics) levels. Since joining National Hispanic University, Vecellio has developed online courses for their MA in education and BA in child development programs. He is a member of the academic advisory council for the San José Job Corps Center and also serves as a member of the Board of Institutional Reviewers for the California Commission on Teacher Credentialing. He may be reached via e-mail at: svecellio@nhu.edu

Noemi Waight is associate professor of science education at the University at Buffalo. Her research focuses on the examination of the life cycles and historical development of technologies as well as the impact on enactment in science classrooms. The writings of philosophy of technology and the inherent nature of technology inform the theoretical framework used in her research work. Her research examines the design, development, implementation, adoption, and enactment of technological tools (e.g., computer-based models, bioinformatics tools, databases) in the context of central, reform-based, K–12 science teaching approaches. Two complementary perspectives guide this research: First, she examines the enactment of technological tools by documenting the full cycle from design and development to actual implementation in science classrooms. Second, to fully understand the implications of this cycle, her research seeks to elucidate the theoretical underpinnings of the nature of technology (NoT) as it pertains to K–12 science education and to empirically examine the factors, conditions, and agencies that impact and mediate enactment of technology in science education. In addition, Waight's work has evolved to examine the role of school leadership and STEM implementation and the role of computer science to facilitate scientific understanding.

Jennifer Wilhelm is associate professor in science education and an engagement and outreach faculty member of the University of Kentucky's Partnership Institute for Mathematics and Science Education Reform. She is also the department chair of the STEM Education Department. She holds an MS in Physics from Michigan State University and a PhD in mathematics/science Education from the University of Texas. Wilhelm's primary research interest involves the design of inquiry-based, project-enhanced, interdisciplinary learning environments. She investigates how people understand science and mathematics concepts as they participate in project work that demands the integration of multiple content areas. Wilhelm's research focuses on project pieces that are inherently interdisciplinary and fruitful for contextualized student learning. Some examples include examining the development of students' science and mathematics content understanding as they engage in studies of motion and rate of change; sound waves and trigonometry; and the moon's phases, the moon's motion, and spatial geometry.

Ara Winter is a data manager at the Bosque Ecosystem Monitoring Program (BEMP) which is a jointing run non-profit between the University of New Mexico (UNM) Department of Biology and Bosque School. As a data manager, he focuses on supporting the data science (statistics, modeling, and curation) needs of BEMP and students and faculty at UNM.

CPSIA information can be obtained
at www.ICGtesting.com
Printed in the USA
LVHW052026060519
616799LV00009B/114/P